Impostor addresses a question that haunts people everywhere: where is God in my struggles? Pulling from the fields of psychology and neurology, and based on her experience working with eating disorders, Schulte shows how we become imprisoned by listening to Satan's lies. With compassion and empathy, she speaks to how fear, loss, anger, helplessness and shame lead us to protect our hearts by building walls against hurt. Most importantly *Impostor* provides a pathway out by providing practical strategies for breaking down and rebuilding walls, discovering truth about who God is and what he offers and growing in relationship with Him. This book is a must read for anyone who is open to seeking God in their journey to freedom.

—CARYLYNN LARSON, PhD
FOUNDER, ROCK RECOVERY & LEADERSHIP COACH,
CREATING OPEN SPACE

Rita shines a bright spotlight on the masks people wear and how "impostors" can threaten spiritual, mental and emotional health. She expertly lays out the information and the tools one can use to banish these masks for good, encourages self-reflection, and for those who've struggled to know who they really are....helps replace the lies with truth.

—KIRSTEN HAGLUND
MISS AMERICA 2008
INTERNATIONAL WOMEN'S EMPOWERMENT SPEAKER
PRESIDENT OF THE KIRSTEN HAGLUND FOUNDATION

D0877462

Rita Schulte is committed to helping people live in unmasked authenticity. The great longing behind this book is to help you become the real deal.

—JOHN ORTBERG
SENIOR PASTOR, MENLO PARK PRESBYTERIAN CHURCH
AUTHOR, *SOUL KEEPING*

As founder at The Center for thirty years we have seen what Rita so carefully shares in these pages how we may truly be blind to those things that bind us up and keep us from truly living the life God has for us of peace and freedom from our past. There is hope and a plan in these pages. Read on for a new vision for your life!

—GREGORY L. JANTZ, PhD
FOUNDER, THE CENTER: A PLACE OF HOPE

impostor

RITA SCHULTE

impostor

Most CHARISMA HOUSE BOOK GROUP products are available at special quantity discounts for bulk purchase for sales promotions, premiums, fund-raising, and educational needs. For details, write Charisma House Book Group, 600 Rinehart Road, Lake Mary, Florida 32746, or telephone (407) 333-0600.

IMPOSTOR by Rita Schulte, LPC
Published by Siloam
Charisma Media/Charisma House Book Group
600 Rinehart Road
Lake Mary, Florida 32746
www.charismahouse.com

Cover design by Lisa Rae Cox
Design Director: Justin Evans

Visit the author's website at http://ritaschulte.com.

Library of Congress Cataloging-in-Publication Data:
Schulte, Rita, 1954-
  Impostor / by Rita Schulte. -- First edition.
    pages cm
  Includes bibliographical references.
  ISBN 978-1-62136-969-1 (trade paper) -- ISBN 978-1-62136-970-7 (e-book)
  1. Christian women--Religious life. 2. Self-esteem in women--Religious aspects--Christianity. 3. Self-actualization (Psychology)--Religious aspects--Christianity. 4. Self-actualization (Psychology) in women. I. Title.
  BV4527.S2775 2014
  248.8'43--dc23
                                        2014024846

This book contains the opinions and ideas of its author. It is solely for informational and educational purposes and should not be regarded as a substitute for professional medical treatment.

People and names in this book are composites created by the author from her experiences as a counselor. Names and

First edition

14 15 16 17 18 — 987654321
Printed in the United States of America

CONTENTS

Acknowledgments.........................xi

Introduction xiii

1 The Secrets We Keep........................1

2 What We Don't Notice Can Hurt Us.........17

3 The Setup 33

4 The Spinning of Our Secret Self..............61

5 Your Brain on God 75

6 Our Unattended Sorrows................... 95

7 The Truth About God......................111

8 Who's Your Daddy? 135

9 The Heart of the Problem 149

10 Rebuilding the Walls 171

11 Practicing the Presence of God............. 193

Notes 217

ACKNOWLEDGMENTS

I WOULD LIKE TO thank Adrienne Gaines and the team at Charisma Media for making this project possible. I would also like to express my gratitude to all the courageous men and women I have sat with over the years who have struggled with disordered eating, depression, and anxiety. You are my heroes.

INTRODUCTION

ARE YOU LIVING the "try hard" life? Do you keep trying harder and harder to be what others want or expect you to be, only to find that the acceptance you crave always seems to be just beyond reach? I meet men and women in this place almost daily in my practice as a therapist. Afraid of being rejected or abandoned, they hide their true selves behind any number of masks to get others' approval.

At some point they became convinced that they were somehow inherently flawed and unlovable. So they created someone who is loveable, a false self they could hide behind. They created an Impostor.

The masks we wear may make it seem as though we have it all together, but eventually we all get tired of pretending. We all want to be loved for who we really are. But where do we start?

In this book I will lead you, the reader, on a journey to break free of the lies keeping the Impostor in place and rediscover who you really are. Our masks may be different—pleaser, performer, controller, perfectionist—but they all stem from the same core struggle: not understanding who we are in Christ. When we don't know who we are, we buy into all types of lies and false beliefs that convince us we're worthless, unlovable, and inadequate.

The good news is that Jesus came to bind up the bro-kenhearted and set us free! But the only way to freedom is to expose our true selves and let Christ do a healing work. Our hearts matter to Him, and if we'll have the courage to press forward, we will discover what it means to find our identity in Christ.

In these pages we'll take a look at the types of masks we've all learned to construct to avoid life's pain and rejection, and we'll trace their origin back to the Garden of Eden where all this mess started with Adam and Eve. We'll learn how our "flesh" (coping strategies) actually helps us in constructing a false self. We'll also look at "needs" and how they drive our behavior and help deter-mine the types of masks we choose to wear. We will look intently at our concept of God because what we believe about Him will determine the course our lives will take. We'll also engage with some real-life individuals who have walked through the valleys of sorrow and suffering, and we'll examine some well-known biblical figures to see firsthand how the masks they wore failed to give them the protection they desired.

At its core this book will help you reconnect with the heart of God, because only there does real and lasting change occur. Head knowledge is great. Counseling tech-niques are helpful. But the journey to discover truth and live authentically will require something more. It will take knowing—knowing God's heart toward us and ours toward Him. As this revelation unfolds, the masks we wear won't be necessary any longer.

To aid in this journey toward healing, I developed

Jesse's story. Though fictional, Jesse is based on real-life conversations and counseling experiences I have had with clients through the years. While Jesse's struggle presents itself through an eating disorder, her experiences will help anyone see why we question who we are and construct masks to hide our true selves.

Getting rid of the Impostors masking your identity will not be easy. It will take intentional effort on your part to ponder the questions at the end of each chapter with brutal honesty. It will take coming face-to-face with your own feelings of inadequacy to experience the inexhaustible sufficiency of Christ that can be manifested in your life. But freedom is worth the effort.

Life can be better, God can feel closer, and you can find the courage to remove the masks you've worn and live from your true identity in Christ. God is faithful, and He will complete the good work He has begun in you. Deuteronomy 31:8 says: "The LORD himself goes before you and will be with you. He will never leave you nor forsake you. Do not be afraid; do not be discouraged." It's time for healing to begin.

Chapter 1
THE SECRETS WE KEEP

I thank God for my handicaps, for through them, I
have found myself, my work and my God.[1]

—HELEN KELLER

JESSE WAS DYING, and we both knew it. While her health certainly wasn't good from all the years of abusing her body through starvation, purging, and chronic dieting, it wasn't her *physical* death that I feared. It was the death of her *heart*. For many years her heart sat frozen beneath layers and layers of countless hurts and unresolved pain. Without rekindling desire from the distant corners of her soul, I knew she didn't have a prayer.

As her therapist, I had been a key player in the metadrama of her life for almost a decade. The consummate encourager, I tried to pour God-sized truths into her wounded heart, hoping that somehow I could convince her of her value and worth. Maybe that was the problem, though. I wasn't the one she needed to hear from—God was, and His voice seemed to be consistently sabotaged by the Impostor that eventually overtook her identity.

There were times when I thought she had given up on life completely, only to see her resurrect her heart once again from the ash heap of loss. Her tenacity amazed me. Slowly she became willing to risk stepping out from behind the shadow of the Impostor she had created in order to find her own identity. This was no easy task. There were days when his voice would overpower her willingness to choose wisely, and her anger would erupt with fury. She blamed herself, she blamed others, and she blamed God.

I remember asking her one day when she decided to stop believing God had a plan for her life. It took a long time for her to find the answer. But together, as we put all the pieces of the puzzle in place, she found more than answers. She found the heart of God.

As for me, I never lost hope she could recover and live the abundant life Christ had designed her to live. I carried that faith for both of us for quite a while.

In truth, Jesse wasn't much different from the many women I have counseled over the years who have struggled with disordered eating and identity issues. She was bright, talented, a perfectionist, and exceptionally beautiful—and everyone noticed. She once told me that by age ten she had already become addicted to the praise and admiration of others. When she entered adolescence, everything she did became centered on being perfect and looking perfect.

It eventually drove her to destruction. By age thirty she had been in and out of more treatment facilities than she cared to remember. Nothing worked. Something was driving her—some secret she seemed afraid to reveal, a secret she said she would never tell anyone.

Until one day she decided to tell me.

COMING OUT OF HIDING

The National Eating Disorders Association estimates there are twenty million American women who suffer from some kind of eating disorder.[2] According to research, anorexia is the third most common chronic illness among adolescents[3] while approximately 80 percent of ten-year-old girls have dieted at least once in their lives.[4]

But people with eating disorders aren't the only ones hiding today. The entire human race hides. Why? Because we all fear rejection, and if we put on a mask and pretend we're perfect, well, maybe no one will notice we're not.

Perhaps we fear exposure. Perhaps we're terrified someone will find out who we really are and leave us. At the heart of the matter, we fear being known—so we hide, and we develop all sorts of coping strategies and call them disorders in an attempt to quiet the silent scream of our own souls.

When does it happen? When does the bottom drop out for someone and lead them into such maladaptive behavior patterns as addictions and eating disorders? Is there a way to predict the fallout and maybe do something on the front end of things to avoid it? How in the world does someone develop an eating disorder—or any other type of disorder for that matter?

The answer to those questions is as complex as the men and women who struggle. But through my years of treating different types of mental health issue—such as eating disorders, low self-esteem, anxiety, depression, and loss issues—I have come to identify some common themes that set the stage for what I call the Impostor, who eventually overtakes a person's identity.

To help you, the reader, understand and deal with these issues as they show up in your own life, we'll explore some of the messages, lies, thinking errors, and other contributing factors that set up this Impostor, or false self, that seeks to replace your true self.

Most importantly you'll learn what it takes to distinguish the Impostor's identity from the one that is intrinsically yours to claim in Christ. Healing will come as you gain the courage to remove the Impostor's mask and begin the journey of self-discovery.

What that means, though, is that you will have to risk coming out of hiding.

TO TELL THE TRUTH

Back in 1956, there was a popular game show on television called *To Tell the Truth*. It ran for about forty-five years in various formats, and I think the idea behind the show fits nicely to set up this whole concept of an Impostor. The show featured a panel of celebrity judges who attempted to identify a described contestant who had an interesting or unusual story. Two other contestants were impostors, pretending to be the original character.

The panel of judges would question the three contestants, and the impostors were allowed to lie to convince the judges they were the real character. However, the central character was sworn to tell the truth about his or her identity. After the questioning was done, the panel voted on who they believed was the "real" character. At the end of the show the host would say, "Will the real (person's name) please stand up?" The central character was then revealed. Prize money was awarded to the challengers based on the number of incorrect votes the impostors could draw.

As I watched clips of some of these old shows, I couldn't help but think about this on a spiritual level. It occurred to me that the only thing that separated the central character from the impostors was a *birthright*. The central character had a birth certificate that confirmed his or her true identity, a document that authenticated who he or she was.

That's what we have as believers. We have a birth certificate that gives us a new identity, one that can never perish, spoil, or fade.

God made provision to take us out of Adam and place us into Christ. He exchanged the old man for the new. This identity that we have been given provides us with everything we need for life. Did you catch that? *Everything.* Not one thing, not some things, not a bunch of things—but everything! We don't have to pretend, and we don't have to perform. It's totally free, and all we have to do is receive it.

You see, in the game show the central character didn't have to do anything to be who he or she claimed to be. All that was necessary was for that person to show up and tell the truth. The impostors, on the other hand, had to pretend. They had to lie. They had to try and imitate the central character, but they were counterfeits. They could have walked like, talked like, dressed like, and copied the central character in every way, shape, or form, but would they ever be the central character? No, because *identity is always determined by birth, not by performance.*

Why is that important for eating-disordered clients—or any of us, for that matter? Because many of us are walking in a false identity, an identity we've created where we have to wear masks and pretend like we have it all together. You see, if we don't know who we are, if we believe we are intrinsically flawed or something is wrong with us, then we will need to create an Impostor or a false self in order to get our needs met. That's what the masquerade is all about, isn't it?

PAPER FACES ON PARADE

In the classic Broadway play *The Phantom of the Opera*, the Phantom is known secretly to the beautiful young chorus girl, Christine Daae, as the Angel of Music. He takes her on as his protégé and teaches her to sing, promising to make her a star. She is drawn to him in an unexplainable way—terrified of him, but compelled to obey his commands. His voice sings songs in her head even as she sleeps, and it whispers to her throughout the day.[5]

The Phantom is a genius at manipulation. He is jealous, mesmerizing, and controlling, and he will settle for no other idols in the life of his victims. He must hide his disfigured face behind a mask because of his own lie-based existence and shame.

There's a particular clip in the movie version of the play that always catches my attention and brings out the counselor in me. It's the masquerade scene. The heart of the song gives us the following messages:

- We must hide our real selves so the world won't know us.
- There are others wearing masks all around us.
- We can fool any of our friends by wearing a mask.

The song reveals something powerful about masks and their ability to conceal one's true identity. It also reveals the motives for donning those masks. The Phantom wore a mask to conceal his disfigurement and to hide from the world. Why was he hiding? Shame. He was different. He was disfigured. He was a horror even to himself. Unlovable. Unacceptable. Rejected.

The Phantom had to create a false persona to deceive Christine. After all, who would love a monster? He desperately needed her love and the security she provided. But in order to get what he needed, he had to hide his real self because he was terrified of rejection.

The Phantom was a magician, and what do magicians do? Deceive. They make us believe something that isn't really true. They're masters at creating illusion. They play with and manipulate your mind.

Does this sound familiar? Whom else do we know who does that? Satan. He masquerades as an angel of light. He pretends to have your best interests at heart. He pretends to meet all your needs. He pretends to be your best friend, but he's just like the Phantom—a liar. Consider what Jesus says of Satan:

> Your father the devil...is a liar and the father of it.
> —JOHN 8:44, NKJV

THE UNEXPECTED PATH OF ESCAPE

How do we dispel lies? How do we break through the present darkness? What broke the Phantom's hold on Christine? How was she able to silence his voice and find her own? Three things: risk, courage, and unfailing love.

Christine found the courage to risk exposing her secret and confronting her fears. Once the secret was out, it no longer had the power to control her. The light exposed the darkness. The truth dispelled fear. Whatever Christine believed would happen as a result of her telling the truth, she was able to face it without being utterly destroyed.

That's the key. Each of us must discover that if we go to those places of emotional pain, we will not be destroyed. So we must learn how to tolerate that which we believe is intolerable in order to find freedom.

The goal of the Phantom was to keep fear alive in Christine's heart so that he could use it to manipulate her. That's what an impostor does, and that's what he did to my friend Jesse for almost twenty-five years. But Christine was courageous. She was afraid to go against the Phantom, but she knew there was no other path to freedom. If you're a believer, you have the power of the indwelling Spirit in you, and greater is He who is in you than He who is in the world.

God loved you so much, He sent His one and only Son to die in your place. This is the story of unfailing love. God loves you just as you are. He doesn't expect you to be perfect.

To stay in the game and fight, to beat the Impostor, you have to believe there is something worth fighting for. That something is your *heart*. And your heart matters to God. How do I know? Because He says so over and over in the Bible. This Jesus, the One who bled and died for you, divinely inspired these words. Take a look:

> Let not your heart be troubled; if you believe in God, believe also in me. In My Father's house are many rooms; if it were not so, I would have told you. I go there to prepare a place for you. And if I go and prepare a place for you, I will come again and receive you to Myself; that where I am there you may be also.
> —JOHN 14:1–3, NKJV

> I have engraved your name on the palms of my hand.
> —ISAIAH 49:16

> For God so loved the world that He gave His only
> begotten Son, that whoever believes in Him should
> not perish but have everlasting life.
>
> —JOHN 3:16, NKJV

If you don't know the wonder of God's unfailing love, if you don't value yourself enough or think you're worth it, He does. Let Him woo you. Let Him show you He cared enough about your heart to take the steel into His hands and feet so you might have a shot at redemption.

The Impostor may seem like a trusted friend on the front end of things, but just as the Phantom turned on Christine, your Impostor will turn on you, wreaking havoc on your mind and in your life until you no longer have any control.

Take the risk that God will meet you right where you are even if you feel like a hot mess. That's where He does His best work—right in the middle of our messes and failures. He gets the glory for resurrecting us. And resurrection is way better than the misery you're living in, trying so hard to make yourself perfect.

Maybe you doubt He's there. Maybe you've never cried out to Him because you figured He'd be just like all the other players in the story. Distant. Detached. Unavailable. But He's not. Scripture says, "The Lord is near" (Phil. 4:5). Take the chance. What if all you needed was right there, only a prayer away, and you didn't see it? What if you really do have *everything* you need for life (2 Pet. 1:3)?

The real challenge—the one I presented to Jesse—was

this question: Can you do the work necessary to find and recognize everything?

WHY THE IMPOSTOR?

Before we can answer the question of what's driving us to create an Impostor, it might be helpful to define the word. According to New Oxford American Dictionary, an *impostor* is "a person who pretends to be someone else in order to deceive others for personal gain."

That tells me there is a payoff to hosting the Impostor. Think again about the game show *To Tell the Truth*. What was the payoff for the game show contestants? What were they trying to do? They didn't just show up on the show for no reason. They showed up with a belief they could win money or prizes.

What's the payoff for my eating-disordered clients? They aren't starving themselves to death, bingeing and purging, overexercising, and all the other things they do for no reason. They do it because they believe that having a thin body will give them value and worth, adequacy and love, acceptance and security. How do they get there? By hiding their true selves. Remember, the words to the song "Masquerade" explain the desire to hide one's real self so that the world won't know.

How do they hide? With the masks they wear.

So let's define the word *mask*. According to the New Oxford American Dictionary, a mask is "any manner or expression that hides one's true character or feelings."

It's a pretense so that you can deceive those who thought they knew you, according to those lyrics again.

Let's analyze the roles these masks play and the pay-offs they provide—not only for those who struggle with eating disorders, but also for all of us who seem to be hiding.

BEHIND THE MASKS WE WEAR

The first thing the masks do is make us look attractive. They have to in order for us to gain the acceptance we need from others. After all, they're designed to make it look like we have it all together.

But behind the masks the Impostor's voice is anything but pretty. Here's how Jesse described the different voices the Impostor used on her:

The Perfectionist/Performer

I can remember trying to be perfect and look perfect from the time I was little. I so wanted everyone to like me. When I messed up, I beat myself up relentlessly. I drove myself to be the best at everything, and if I wasn't, I would try harder.

There is so much pressure out there to be perfect. We're bombarded with messages that say "You're deficient." The solution? Try harder.

The "Try Harder"

Trying hard became a way of life for me. Because I was so unsure of who I was, I looked to others to define me. I thought if I could just keep trying hard enough, one day

I would be good enough. I felt so much self-loathing. My life became a living hell. It seemed no amount of trying was good enough anymore, so I just gave up.

The Controller

I spent hours counting how many calories I'd taken in. I weighed and measured what I ate. I weighed myself all day long. If I cheated and ate something I wasn't supposed to, I was compelled to go to the gym for hours and punish myself. I was so exhausted! Being in control was the only thing that mattered. It made me feel safe. Everything was so out of control in my life, and the eating disorder was the one thing I could control. It was the one friend I had. I knew it carried strict rules, but if I followed them, I believed all would be OK.

The Pleaser

I would do anything not to make waves. When I walked into a room I'd do an audience analysis, and I would say and do whatever people needed me to say or do in order to be well liked and popular. I couldn't say no. I couldn't risk someone saying anything bad about me, so I would do anything to avoid that. I never knew who I was because I was so busy trying to be what everyone else thought I should be. I was stuck. Frozen. I had no identity of my own.

The Conflict-Avoider

I hated conflict! I found it so uncomfortable. I would just withdraw or do whatever people wanted me to do to avoid it. I remember once when I was really upset at my best friend, and I couldn't tell her how much she hurt me, even though she was my best friend. I believed I couldn't make waves, or others wouldn't like me.

The Fixer

I felt responsible for making everyone happy. I spent years trying to solve and fix everyone's problems. I couldn't stand to see anyone hurting or in pain. I think I got my need for value and worth by always being everyone's rescuer.

EMPTY PROMISES

As you can see, this is an exhausting way to live! So why do it? What is the payoff? What does the Impostor promise?

Here's the truth: All of our behavior is purpose driven. We don't generally do anything without some kind of reward or payoff. We said earlier that there were payoffs for wearing the Impostor's masks. So what are they?

The main payoff is to help us avoid pain and rejection. That's the main goal of our flesh. Dr. Larry Crabb weighs in about the purpose and payoffs of wearing masks in his book *Fully Alive*:

> The masks we wear, the fig leaves we clothe our-selves with, the personas we present to others to make sure they never have reasonable grounds to criticize or reject us, and the secrets we keep to preserve a favorable social image—they're all designed to keep a terrible fear at bay and to numb the pain of impending soul-death that threatens to

destroy us. They keep us alone, feeling unwanted and disrespected as we go about our lives.[6]

If our core fear is being known, the Impostor's goal is to help make sure we aren't. By doing so, he can keep us isolated and maintain control over us, just as the Phantom did with Christine. By using this terrible fear that threatens to overwhelm us, the Impostor shames us into silence and secrecy. We come to believe, "I can't tell you my story, and I won't tell you my story, because if you really knew me, you would surely reject me. So I have to keep the messy part of my life a secret because I am ashamed of who I am."

We don't want to face what we feel because our feelings expose the beliefs we have about the condition of our hearts. But our feelings are good indicators that something is going on inside that needs tending: a wounded heart. Instead of trying to change them, instead of burying them, instead of trying to pretend we're doing great, we would be wise to listen to them because they hold the keys that can unlock the sorrows of our lives. They can allow us space to face our fears, grieve our losses, and wrestle with God.

Another way the Impostor keeps us self-sufficient is by having us depend on the masks. If I'm depending on the masks, whom am I *not* depending on? Christ. Being self-sufficient allows us to keep God at a manageable distance so He won't mess up our lives.

The truth is, we're afraid God might require something of us that we may just not be ready to surrender.

An eating disorder? Anger? Unforgiveness? A besetting sin? A rebellious heart? Rest assured, you and I can't move through a moment without trusting in someone or something, and it will either be Christ or it will be the Impostor. What's his hook? "I can meet all your needs."

We do a pretty good job believing him too—but should we?

CONSIDER THIS

- What masks have you worn in an attempt to find value and worth (Pleaser, Controller, Perfectionist)?

- What types of behaviors do these masks generate in your life (can't say no, have to do everything right, disordered eating issues, etc.)?

- What is the payoff for you in wearing these masks (getting others' approval, feeling secure, feeling adequate)?

- What fears are you currently dealing with?

- What are you afraid to surrender to the Lord? Why?

- What false beliefs have you bought into that have stolen your true identity?

Chapter 2
WHAT WE DON'T NOTICE CAN HURT US

Give sorrow words; the grief that does not speak knits
up the o-er wrought heart and bids it break.[1]
—WILLIAM SHAKESPEARE, *MACBETH*

ANY NOTABLE AUTHORS have written on the subject of eating disorders, and just as many have said, "It's not about the food!" I wholeheartedly agree. But if it's not about the food, what is it about? Those who struggle can't even understand their actions in totality. Simultaneously their loved ones' lack of knowledge and understanding of what would drive someone to intentionally destroy themselves is equally perplexing.

I taught Jesse a lot of truth over the years we worked together. Some days she was able to muddle through; other days were like trudging through wet cement. But what really helped Jesse was teaching her about needs and how they are linked to our coping strategies and belief systems. I helped her understand our five most basic core needs as humans. She soon began to see that starving herself was, in part, a way to get each of those needs met.

Jesse's beliefs about her appearance told her that in order to be loved, acceptable, secure, valuable, and adequate, she must be thin. She was shocked to realize how the eating disorder provided a sense of security for her by meeting these needs. She started to notice that being thin and pretty attracted attention, male and female. This caused her to develop a false sense of security. Because her parents placed so much emphasis on appearance, Jesse came to believe she was valuable only if she looked perfect.

Eventually, though, Jesse began evaluating the cost of her eating disorder. She began to question the cost of this so-called security she had hung on to for so long. Her evaluations led her to consider the possibility that the security the eating disorder provided was really an illusion. After all these years she still felt empty and insecure.

OUR CORE NEEDS

So, what are these needs the Impostor promises to meet, and why are they so important? They're important because our needs create drives within us that compel us to behave in ways we believe will fill us. Needs are essential for life, and without them we won't function as God created us to function.

Our physical needs are pretty straightforward: food, water, air, and shelter. Without them we will die. But our soul's needs often remain hidden and known only by the heart. Their loss creates the loss of a different kind: the death of our hearts.

Take a look at the needs listed below along with their definitions and consider how the masks you're wearing may be striving to meet one—or all—of these needs:

- Love: unconditional caring from another

- Acceptance: feeling affirmed just as I am

- Value and worth: my meaning and purpose in life

- Security: freedom from harm and emotional safety

- Adequacy: the belief that I am OK, capable, and adequate

Kim was a former client of mine who gave me permission to tell a small piece of her story in my book *Shattered: Finding Hope and Healing Through the Losses of Life.* I use her story here because it is a good example of how living without what we need affects our hearts. Here's part of her story:

> Kim was sitting in the chair across from me, but her expression told me that her mind had transported her somewhere else. She was staring blankly into space, almost not able to process what I was saying. Perhaps it was uncertainty I saw, or perhaps it was sadness. I could see she was trying to grasp it, thinking that if she could somehow unlock the door of her heart, it would set her free. Then a crystallizing moment occurred for her and she said, "I never knew it was okay for me to have a need and actually express it. All these years I have buried that part of myself, fearful of what might happen if I actually dared to voice desire."[2]

Kim spent her entire life starving herself because she felt unlovable, insecure, and inadequate. She withdrew, shut down, and built walls around heart because she was afraid to use her voice to express desire. Because she was terrified of being rejected, she looked to an eating disorder, an Impostor, to get a sense of life.

Kim is only one of countless clients I've treated who sit behind the mask of broken dreams and unmet expectations—people who allow their unmet needs to percolate below the conscious surface, protesting in the form of eating disorders, anxiety and depression, and substance abuse problems.

Many of us have chosen to deaden desire and refuse to need. Why? Because it's safer that way—or so we think. Better not to risk. We'd rather do anything than be disappointed for the millionth time, so we wall off our hearts to what's essential for life.

But we find that the ache of the soul will not be silenced. Without a secure sense of identity the self responds by looking to whoever or whatever will fill what remains lacking. If your needs have gone unmet, you have experienced loss, and if enough loss goes unchecked, it will cause you to create an Impostor.

THE ART OF NOTICING

Unmet needs create a loss or a deficit. My job as Jesse's therapist was to help her develop an awareness of this needs piece. To do that, I taught Jesse the art of noticing.

Noticing involves paying attention to both our inner

and outer worlds. The external world is constantly offering information to us. We scan that information from sources like television, the Internet, newspapers, and our personal relationships. All that information affects us on an internal level—the heart level. Whether we've had a fight with our spouse, heard about a terrorist attack, or seen a message on TV about how we should look, all of it impacts what's going on inside us. The problem is, most of us don't pay close attention to our inner world. We get the external information, and we don't address how it's impacted us.

Because we are three-dimensional beings—body, soul, and spirit—everything that happens to us affects each part. The external world makes us task-oriented, so it's easy to get sidetracked or detached from our inner life. Either we're too busy to take the time to notice, or we are *afraid* to take the time. Ignoring our inner life can cause the losses in our lives to build up and create a tension and pressure that can cause us to lose heart.

That's why I taught Jesse to begin to pay attention to how her physical body handled stress. I taught her how to do a body scan to assess her tension. I had her sit for a couple minutes each day, several times a day, and close her eyes. I asked her to key in, starting with her head, on each part of her body, looking for signals like tight muscles, a knot in her stomach, feelings of anxiety, or anything else that popped up. This is a simple but powerful exercise.

Getting in touch with those places of stress and tension in our bodies allows us to take it a step further and analyze if there is any correlation between our bodily stress and our internal world. Often Jesse would notice a knot in her stomach and tension in her neck and shoulders when she felt a loss of one of her core needs. For example, we identified that when she stepped on the scale and could physically see she had gained weight, she would begin to feel insecure and inadequate. In time she became adroit at seeing her triggers and, using abdominal breathing techniques and muscle relaxation, at calming herself and sitting with uncomfortable emotions.

Once she had all that down, I asked her to begin paying attention to three important things as they related to her needs being met:

- When she was trying to get one of the five needs met

- When she was feeling a loss of one of those needs

- What she did behaviorally in response to each of those scenarios

I wanted Jesse to pay attention to how she coped when she felt a loss of a need or was trying to get a need met. If she was trying to win the approval of others, what masks did she notice she was pulling out of the drawer in order to feel acceptable or adequate? Was it the pleaser, the controller, the avoider? If she had a fight with her spouse and felt a loss of security, what did she do? Did she restrict more, exercise more, withdraw emotionally?

I wanted Jesse to notice what needs were driving her behavior. Remember—all our behavior is purpose driven. When she looked to the masks instead of looking to Christ, she was walking in a false identity. When that happened, she was being robbed moment by moment of her true identity in Christ.

LOSS OF IDENTITY

Dr. Trisha Gura says in her book *Lying in Weight: The Hidden Epidemic of Eating Disorders in Adult Women*, "To become a woman a girl must develop an identity, a self that abides no matter what."[3] Peggy Claude Pierre, director of Montreux, an eating disorder clinic in Victoria, Canada, and author of the book *The Secret Language of Eating Disorders*, echoes Gura's sentiments, saying, "To recover from anorexia the victim must first develop a sense of self before she can address her self-esteem."[4]

As I was reading Dr. Gura's book, I came across a really sad story. It was about a young girl named Jenny Lauren, the niece of fashion icon Ralph Lauren. Let's see to how the Impostor robbed Jenny of her identity:

> Dolled up in gray flannel Bermudas and a purple Shetland sweater, her hair partly swept up, Jenny swaggered down the runway, 7 years old, pouty and seductive. She gave the audience an angelic vision. Her father, head of Men's Design at Polo Ralph Lauren, was so proud. Her famous uncle was awestruck. After the show, Ralph told his brother that Jenny "was the most beautiful creature he had ever laid eyes on." A girl goddess.

She never forgot that moment, or the urge to re-create it. She tried to, many times… Finally, the pressure to have the perfect body became so great so early in her life that she fought back with what amounted to a vow to starve herself.

By 10, she developed anorexia; by 15, bulimia. She entered a catastrophic cycle of bingeing and purging through vomiting, laxatives, running, gym workouts, and exercise classes. By 24, she had so abused her body that her upper bowel broke loose and wedged in the space between her vagina and her anus….

Until recently, she had no energy left to put into the hard work of finding new ways to handle adult situations, such as who she was underneath the image of "girl goddess." In a dark way, her eating disorder served a purpose [payoff]: by getting sick, Jenny found a way to flee the pressure and hide backstage.[5]

Overtaking a person's identity is no easy task, so the Impostor must work especially hard in the beginning to win our trust and make us believe he's safe—when he's anything but. An enemy of our soul, he comes masquerading as an angel of light, challenging us at the core of our identity. For a young girl like Jenny Lauren who was struggling to figure out the messy business of adolescence and gain a sense of value and worth, let's just say she was easy prey.

The labels of performance and perfection became the masks Jenny wore for years because she believed they would meet her needs for life. It drove her to destruction.

Her behaviors grew so out of control that she stifled any chance of normal childhood development. She so desperately wanted to keep up the image. Why? It met her needs. But that didn't solve the greater issue of identity development, a task she failed to complete.

Many of us are so busy trying to be someone that we don't create our own identities. We're not authentic to our own selves. We don't listen to our own voices, and we certainly aren't listening to God's. The masks we wear are the ones we believe others need us to wear in order to be acceptable.

In his book *The Blessing,* my friend Dr. John Trent shares the story of his first day as an intern at a psychiatric hospital that would forever leave a haunting impression on him. He stood watch over a handsome, well-mannered, highly intelligent young man who had tried to commit suicide. The boy had been a straight-A student his entire life but failed to get an A in a tennis class. This plunged him into deep despair. As the young man shared his story, Dr. Trent learned that the boy's father had been a highly driven, brilliant, and demanding man who expected nothing but perfection from his son. The boy had never been affirmed or blessed by his father. What a travesty that he would have chosen death over facing his dad with a less-than-perfect performance.[6]

This young man, like so many of us, put his source of value in someone else's opinion of what he should do and how he should perform. Don't get me wrong—there is nothing wrong with a parent wanting their child to do well in life. But when that desire becomes a goal that's unbalanced, it can mortally wound a child/adolescent.

If we put our source of value in whatever other people think or believe about us, be it our appearance, IQ, personality, success, or performance, it's always up for grabs. We have to look a certain way, wear certain clothes, weigh a certain amount, exercise all the time, get perfect grades, never make a mistake, and be a success all the time. Why? Because our belief system tells us if we can actually pull that act off, then life and the potential trials and suffering that come along with it won't overtake us. That leaves us having to control, orchestrate, and manipulate everyone around us. The question is, how well is that working for us?

If, however, we shift our source of value to Christ, it's no longer up for grabs anymore because Jesus said if we choose to depend on Him moment by moment, He'll meet all our needs. That's in cement. Take a look at the following verses:

> God will meet all your needs according to the riches of his glory in Christ Jesus.
> —PHILIPPIANS 4:19

> I can do all things through Christ who strengthens me.
> —PHILIPPIANS 4:13, NKJV

> The LORD will guide you always; he will satisfy your needs in a sun-scorched land and will strengthen your frame.
> —ISAIAH 58:11

For in Christ all the fullness of Deity lives in bodily form, and you have been brought to fullness. He is the head over every power and authority

—COLOSSIANS 2:9

ASK AND YOU WILL RECEIVE

Just like my friend Kim, many of us have trouble asking other people for what we need. Once Kim understood the power that was available to her through the indwelling Holy Spirit, though, all that changed. Let's see how it changes from one of the stories Jesus tells:

Then Jesus said to them, "Suppose you have a friend, and you go to him at midnight and say, 'Friend, lend me three loaves of bread; a friend of mine on a journey has come to me, and I have no food to offer him.'

"And suppose the one inside answers, 'Don't bother me. The door is already locked, and my children and I are in bed. I can't get up and give you anything.' I tell you, even though he will not get up and give you the bread because of friendship, yet because of your shameless audacity he will surely get up and give you as much as you need.

"So I say to you: Ask and it will be given to you; seek and you will find; knock and the door will be opened to you. For everyone who asks receives; the one who seeks finds; and to the one who knocks, the door will be opened. Which of you fathers, if your son asks for a fish, will give him a snake instead? Or if he asks for an egg, will give him a scorpion? If you then, though you are evil, know how to give good gifts to your children, how much more will your Father in heaven give the Holy Spirit to those who ask him!"

—LUKE 11:5–13

This is a remarkable parable, but most of us miss the enormity of what God is trying to show us here. Jesus is teaching on prayer, and He used this story to show us that we need to be bold and persistent in asking God for what we need. He wants to give us good gifts. God is our Father, and even if we were blessed enough to have wonderful earthly fathers, they are still prone to walk in the flesh. Observe: "If *you* [an earthly father] then, *though you are evil*, know how to give good gifts to your children, how much more will your Father in heaven give the Holy Spirit to those who ask him!"

Here's what we see from this passage:

- Earthly fathers, despite their flesh, are still ready to care for and supply the needs of their children.

- God is far more able to meet our needs than anyone else.

- God desires that we rush into His arms and ask for what we need.

- We must speak boldly in our asking.

- We must be persistent in our pleas.

- God gives us the source for *all* that we will ever need through the Holy Spirit.

My client Kim needed comfort. She needed guidance. She needed love. She needed all her needs met, only she didn't understand that everything she needed for life, she already possessed within her through the transforming power of the Holy Spirit. She just never asked because she didn't understand the power. She didn't understand she was supposed to come boldly before the throne of grace and ask a loving Father for what her wounded heart needed.

Beloved, God gave us *the* source. Whatever you ask for (according to His will), He gives through the Holy Spirit. He gives wisdom for any situation. Guidance for all our problems. Comfort for all our sorrows. Out of the Holy Spirit comes the fruit of all things because He lives within us.

Stop right here. Put the book down and breathe that in. Jesus said:

> Unless I go away, the Advocate will not come to you; but if I go, I will send him to you.
> —John 16:7

> If anyone is thirsty, let him come to me and drink. Whoever believes in me, as the Scripture has said, rivers of living water will flow from within him.
> —John 7:37–38

> All this I have spoken while still with you. But the Advocate, the Holy Spirit, will teach you all things and will remind you of everything I have said to you.
> —John 14:25–26

God the Father is able to do exceedingly abundantly more than we can ever ask or imagine through the power of the Holy Spirit. That's why He has placed within us the third person of the Trinity. He knew we would have our hearts shattered along this journey of life. He knew we would need Him. So He put His very life inside us. We have everything we need. We only have to ask!

Satan is not unaware of the needs of our flesh, so he lures us with the things of the world, using the Impostor as his mouthpiece. He convinces us the things of this world will fill us. Listen to John's warning, though:

> Do not love the world or anything in the world. If anyone loves the world, love for the Father is not in them. For everything in the world—the lust of the flesh, the lust of the eyes, and the pride of life—comes not from the Father but from the world. The world and its desires pass away, but whoever does the will of God lives forever.
> —1 JOHN 2:15–17

If you've been wearing masks for a while by now you've probably realized that sooner or later the Impostor will turn on you, demanding, controlling, and orchestrating every move you make until one day you wake up and realize you've lost yourself at the expense of his empty promises. You still feel shame. You're still unhappy. You still feel fat. You're still broken. And you still feel very much alone.

While the Impostor promises control, as we saw in Jenny Lauren's story, that control is only an illusion. It starts out subtly—maybe we just want to lose a few pounds, calm that anxiety, or make that one bet—but after a while it takes on an identity of its own and we're not in control of anything anymore. The promise of a payoff to meet our needs is empty. Jenny Lauren still felt empty, alone, broken, and undone. It was all a deception—a deception that started two thousand years ago in a beautiful garden.

CONSIDER THIS

- What masks have you worn in the name of getting your needs met?

- What have you looked to in order to get a sense of value/worth (appearance, body image, job, success)?

- Do you need the approval of others? If so, what happens when you don't get it?

- How has the loss of getting your needs met by the significant people in your world affected you?

- What false idols have you erected in order to get your need for security met?

- Spend some time reflecting on the five core needs of the heart. Notice how you cope when you feel a loss of one of them—love, acceptance, value and worth, security, or adequacy. Do you withdraw, try harder, avoid, or something else?

Chapter 3
THE SETUP

The thief comes to steal and kill and destroy: I have
come that they may have life and have it to the full.
—JOHN **10:10**

BEING KNOWN IS a scary prospect for most of us, but especially for those who struggle with food issues. Shame and guilt compel them to hide.

But long before any of us decided that secrecy was the best solution to guilt and shame, a couple other folks were busy writing the playbook for hide and seek. Consider Adam and Eve. They enjoyed intimate fellowship with God. They had walked naked, unashamed, and fully known by Him—but one day all that changed.

We all know the story. There were two trees. One life. One death. There was one rule. Don't touch the tree of the knowledge of good and evil. God gave them everything else. Lest we miss it, they lived in *paradise*. Have you ever been to paradise? A vacation, maybe Hawaii or some exotic island where you decided then and there you had died and gone to heaven? You never wanted to leave. Close your eyes for a moment and think about that. Paradise. Imagine it. Sense it. Envision it.

Well, that's nothing compared to what they had. Not only did they dwell in paradise, but they also had an experiential knowing of life moment by moment spent walking with God.

But it wasn't enough. They wrecked it because they wanted what they didn't have. One thing. One temptation. One mistake. It cost us everything.

After their disobedience they heard the sound of the Lord walking in the garden in the cool of the day, searching for them. This day they were hiding because they knew they had disappointed God. They had doubted His character, they had doubted His goodness, and they had believed the lie that they were somehow lacking something that if they just had it, they'd be OK. When they were found, they responded in their flesh the only way they knew how: by blaming, hiding, and performing.

> But the LORD God called to the man, "Where are you?"
>
> He answered, "I heard you in the garden, and I was afraid because I was naked; so I hid."
>
> And he said, "Who told you that you were naked? Have you eaten from the tree that I commanded you not to eat from?" The man said, "The woman you put here with me—she gave me some fruit from the tree, and I ate it."
>
> —GENESIS 3:9–12

It's interesting to note that Adam and Eve had never experienced the emotions of shame, guilt, insecurity, or inadequacy before that moment. They were created by God to lack *nothing*. In order to manage their negative emotions, they had to do something to protect themselves from being seen, known, and possibly rejected by God.

BELIEVING THE LIE

The real travesty of the Genesis story is that Adam and Eve were already *full*. God had designed it that way. He had given them *everything* that was needed for life. But they let their feelings determine their reality.

Sound familiar? Isn't that what we all do? Because we feel a certain way, we make it a fact. We don't stop to check out the evidence that may or may not support our beliefs. The problem is this: *The interpretations we make about our feelings lead us to develop core beliefs and systems about ourselves, God, and others—many of which are lies.* This is important because our actions always follow our beliefs, and if we believe lies, we'll never walk in the freedom and rest God has for us.

Remember what Eve said to God in Genesis 3: "The serpent *deceived* me, and I ate." Eve felt bad—confused, maybe angry—when Satan told her God was holding out on her by not allowing her to eat of the tree of the knowledge of good and evil. So she made an interpretation about her feelings and reasoned that maybe God wasn't good. Maybe He didn't have her best interests at heart. Maybe she *was* really lacking something she needed. Eating from the tree was a result of her beliefs about God's goodness and her own inadequacy.

Satan's greatest tool against us is deception. Why? Because once you believe the lie—any lie about who you are, just like Eve—you're doomed. Eve believed she was somehow inadequate the way she was. Her desire to be like God, having the knowledge of both good and evil, led her and Adam to separation from God. It led to the loss of their true identity.

Once they lost that, they had no other choice but to construct the mask. The Bible has a special word for the masks we wear. It comes from the Greek word *sarx*, which means *flesh*. And we aren't talking skin and bones in this context. Flesh is the self-life—the life we live apart from God. It helps us hide. It tells us we're OK. It stands opposed to Christ. It's all the strategies you and I use to solve our problems and avoid pain and rejection. You might call these strategies your defense mechanisms.

Here's how Paul describes it:

> Not many of you were wise by human standards; not many were influential; not many were of noble birth.
>
> —1 CORINTHIANS 1:26

> If someone else thinks they have reasons to put confidence in the flesh, I have more: circumcised on the eighth day, of the people of Israel, of the tribe of Benjamin, a Hebrew of Hebrews; in regard to the law, a Pharisee; as for zeal, persecuting the church; as for righteousness based on the law, faultless. But whatever were gains to me I now consider loss for the sake of Christ.
>
> —PHILIPPIANS 3:4–7

What has the evil one convinced you of? What lies might you believe that are keeping you in bondage to your eating disorder or whatever else has taken up the central focus of your life, and at what cost? Is it a troubled marriage, a wayward child, a substance problem that you can't shake? Whatever it is, it's caused you to believe lies about yourself and about God.

If Eve were in the garden today, struggling with an eating disorder, here's what her conversation with Satan might look like. See if you can relate:

> Satan: Has God said you can eat from any tree in the garden?
>
> Eve: From any of the trees in the garden we may eat freely, but we shall not eat from the tree in the middle of the garden, or we will die.
>
> Satan: You surely will not die! For God knows that if you eat from those trees, you'll become fat, lazy, and unproductive. But if you eat from the tree in the middle of the garden, you will be thin, beautiful, and as wise as God forever.
>
> Eve: Hmm, I'm lacking something—a thinner body. If I just had a thinner body, I'd be perfect. I'd probably get that cover shot on the *Tree of Life* magazine I wanted so much. Maybe God's withholding from us. Maybe He isn't as good as we thought. If He was good, He surely wouldn't want us to be unhappy.

The enemy of your soul has convinced you of some powerful lies, all of which involve your performance, appearance, and identity. You obviously believe you're lacking something you need in order to be OK. Look at the list below and see if you can identify anything that fits your experience:

- I need to be thinner.
- I need to be prettier.
- I need to be smarter.
- I must be perfect.
- I should be more outgoing.
- I need to be less outgoing.
- I must have a boyfriend.
- I need to be popular.
- I need to have the right clothes.
- I have to have the right career to be a success.
- I must have a certain home.
- I should be nice to everyone.
- I need everyone to like me.
- I must be a success.
- I need to have a firmer butt, tighter abs, and lose ten pounds.

The lies aren't always outlandish—that's the hook. Isn't it OK to be popular, dress nicely, have a nice house, and have everybody like you? What's wrong with that? Nothing really—unless it's become life for you.

Remember, Satan masquerades as an angel of light. The fruit on the tree looked good. It was pleasing to the eye, or else Eve wouldn't have been tempted to eat it. And so we take the hook. We focus on doing rather than being. Eve wanted to have knowledge. She wanted to be like God. But God had already made her and Adam in His image. They had everything they needed for life. They were full and didn't even realize it.

So to cover their shame, they had to do something. They bought into "if only" thinking and believing. *If only* you were like God. *If only* you were smarter, prettier, thinner, more lovable, more adequate…and the list goes on and on. Instead of walking in the truth of who they were by birthright, Adam and Eve sold it all for a bite of an apple.

As I stated earlier, the most important thing for us to grasp is this: Identity is not determined by performance but by birthright. God breathed His very life into Adam. Adam was full and complete because God decreed it. Likewise, our birth into Christ removes us from our old identity in Adam and places us into Christ—and the two are mutually exclusive. We can't have two identities. One has to go, and that one is the Impostor.

> But God, being rich in mercy, because of His great
> love with which He loved us, even when we were

> dead in our transgressions, made us alive together
> with Christ (by grace you have been saved), and
> raised us up with Him, and seated us with Him in
> the heavenly places in Christ Jesus.
>
> —EPHESIANS 2:4–6, NAS

Think back to the last chapter and my client Kim. Then think about the story of Jenny Lauren. Now think about the story of Adam and Eve. What's the takeaway in all these stories? Here are a few things to consider:

- All of them took the hook.
- All of them believed lies about self, God, and others.
- The payoffs to meet their needs were deceptive.
- Shame caused them to hide their true selves.

Eve vowed to be like God. Jenny vowed to be a girl goddess—at whatever expense. Kim vowed never to ask anyone for anything. Shame causes us to keep secrets and make vows that can radically impact our entire life trajectory. Larry Crabb says, "With our masks, fig leaves, personas, and secrets all well-positioned, we live not to reveal the God of love by the way we relate, but to hide from the fear that threatens to destroy us—our core terror."[1]

If you're looking to any of these worldly things to establish your identity, you're on the performance treadmill, and you'll never find out who you *really* are. Each performance strategy only serves to strengthen the flesh, solidify the Impostor's identity, and lead us further and further away from dependence on God. If whatever you're struggling with has caused you to live a life of shame, if you have been rejected and trust is difficult for you, this will make coming out of hiding all the more difficult.

It's hard to relinquish control if we don't trust. That's why it will be critical for you to find someone you *do* trust to tell your story to, someone who will walk alongside you and listen without trying to fix you. Here are some questions to consider:

- Am I willing to take a risk?

- Are my current strategies getting me what I want?

- How well is what I'm doing working for me?

- Am I living an abundant life?

- Have I counted the cost of my eating disorder? If so, what have I lost?

In the end, only one thing is necessary to begin the healing journey of the heart. It's what I told Jesse over and over: You have to *choose* to live.

She agreed, but she had a few questions about how it all got started. If you're ready for that, read on!

The Science of Attachment

If Adam and Eve started this whole mess, then mom and dad finished us off. But before you go after them, let's have a lesson in attachment theory and brain neurobiology. Let's look at the cutting-edge research that's out there to help us understand why we love, think, and behave the way we do.

It's pretty obvious people don't just wake up one day and decide to develop an eating disorder or any other mental health issue. So how does it all begin? Where does it all begin? Attachment theory, along with brain neurobiology, gives us a great lens of understanding for how and why we're set up to construct an Impostor in the first placed.

Attachment theory is a theory of relationships. The closest kind of relationships. Parent/child. Husband/wife. And most importantly, our relationship with God. If we look at Genesis 2, we see that God is social in His nature and orientation. We see it in the Trinity, the creation of angels, and the creation of man. In Genesis 1 we notice that as God was creating the universe, He consistently used the phrase "It was good" after He created something.

But there was one thing in the garden God said *wasn't* good, and that was that man was alone:

> The Lord God said, "It is not good for man to be alone. I will make a helper suitable for him."
> —Genesis 2:18

This was the birth of relationship. What we see is that the same desire that was in the heart of God, He put in the heart of man. We were created for relationship because that's where we experience being known, and we thrive as we walk in the confines of a safe, secure, and loving connection.

Attachment theory helps us answer the questions "Who am I? Am I loved, am I valued, and is my attachment figure sufficiently near, responsive, and attuned to me?" Thousands of times in our first few years of life these questions are being answered on a daily basis, and how a child learns to deal with his or her emotions rides on the beliefs about his parents' emotional attunement and availability.

So, if the answer to those attachment questions is consistently yes, a child will develop a sense of felt security and will be able to launch out and explore the world around her with a secure attachment. But if the answer to those questions is consistently no, if her parents are dismissive, absent, or harsh, the child will develop some defenses to protest the loss of secure connection—things like anxiety, fear, and anger.

Attachment carries with it some central tenets, so let me give them to you by way of an illustration. I have an old home video movie of my son and me in the park. Michael is about five years old, and he's busy playing and exploring his world on the playground. His ability to do that is predicated on his belief that if anything happens to upset him, he can look back to me, and if anything happens to *really* upset him, he can run to me. I become for him a secure base.

As he's sliding down the slide, something happens. He hits his head and comes running around the slide looking for me. This is classic proximity seeking (that's what we call it when we run to attachment figure for comfort). He runs to me, I embrace him and kiss his head, and you can see a smile come over his little face. You can see he is being comforted and soothed. He gets calm, and then he resumes his play and exploration.

Now, what would happen if I were dismissive or harsh toward him? If I said, "Stop whining. Don't be a baby— big boys don't cry. Go play and stop bothering me!" What's he going to do? How will that affect his heart? He might cry more. He might throw a tantrum to protest my disinterest. He might internalize it all, hang his head, and go away feeling ashamed. The key is this: When the stresses of life weigh down on us, when we're afraid, when there is trouble, the attachment behavioral system is activated and the need for secure connection becomes salient and compelling.

Furthermore, the loss of my attachment figure causes anxiety, grief, and despair. Think about how you've felt if you've lost someone very close to you.

Why is all this so important? Why am I belaboring this? Because it's through this attachment process between mother and child that a child's brain learns to organize itself. The messages we get about who we are shape our identity, form our core belief systems, and help us learn to regulate our emotional responses. The bottom line is that a child learns to see himself through what he witnesses in the parents' responses toward him.

As you're thinking about this, think about your relationship with God. We'll see later that He is our ultimate attachment figure, and we'll consider why our hearts may possibly be shut down to Him because of what mom or dad did or didn't do.

All of this is illustrated beautifully in the movie *Hope Floats* with Sandra Bullock. Let me set it up for you. Sandra Bullock plays Birdie, a young wife who finds out about her husband's infidelity with her best friend on a daytime television talk show. She is devastated. Bernice, the couple's young daughter who was once the apple of her daddy's eye, is faced with the harsh reality that her parents are getting a divorce. Her father comes to the house to ask Bullock for the divorce. Little Bernice wants to go to live with her daddy. She packs her bag and runs outside after her father, who proceeds to tell her that although he loves her, he has no room for her in his life with his soon-to-be new wife.

Here's what he says: "Bernice, you know I'd take you with me if I could, but Connie and I, we need this time to try to make a go of it. Then I'll come back for you; I promise. I promise."[2]

Bernice begs her father to take her, reminding him of the letter he wrote telling her how much he wanted her with him. He tells her that as soon as he's settled with his new wife, he'll come back for her. She breaks down, sobbing hysterically that her daddy doesn't want her, and she runs after him screaming as he drives away.

The scene from this movie exemplifies the idea that secure base scenarios unfold around emotionally charged events, and how a parent helps a child deal with strong emotions becomes critical because the brain is continually recording these scenarios and helping the child draw conclusions about herself. What I am saying here is that neural networks are being established by and through our interactions with the significant attachment figures in our lives, and these interactions are literally shaping our brain.

The problem is that insecure attachment becomes fertile ground for believing lies about self, God, and the world around us. How might little Bernice come to see herself over the next ten or fifteen years? What needs might she feel a loss of here? What core beliefs might take shape in her heart as a result of this interaction with her father? What might Bernice do to cope with her feelings of not being wanted? Wear masks? Construct an Impostor? Could she develop an eating disorder? What lies will she believe the next time someone says to her, "I promise"?

The genesis of the theory

"I hate my life. Correction—I hate myself. I've done nothing, I am nothing, and God has abandoned me." How did Jesse get these messages? How could I help her change or modify these existing beliefs? Who were the major players in her life that helped form these belief systems?

While the culture has proven to be a powerful force

in influencing thoughts and feelings about body image, identity, and self-esteem, as we've learned, families are the major players for the shaping of lives and belief systems for children.

According to John Bowlby, the father of attachment theory, a child learns and develops most optimally in the context of a loving, safe, and secure environment. We get that. This idea is not a new one and has sparked the interest of researchers and psychiatrists for decades. Many noticed that children who were not nurtured did not thrive.

It wasn't until the 1940s, however, that a cohesive set of ideas began to be formulated about the significance of our earliest relationships and their impact. Dr. John Bowlby, a British psychiatrist, spent a good deal of time observing and working with young children in orphanages after World War II. His experiences led him to develop a masterful theory of relationships that came to be known as *attachment theory*. Bowlby believed that the quality of connection to significant loved ones and/or the loss/deprivation of that connection were key to the development of personality and to an individual's subsequent habitual patterns of relatedness with others.

Beliefs about the emotional attunement, availability, and responsiveness of the caregiver impact the child's trajectory throughout her lifespan. In other words, the messages children get about who they are, who they are in relationship to others, and their competency to gain the love they need form an "internal working model," or belief system, of self, God, and the world around them.

It is here they are learning to love and be loved; whether relationships are warm, safe, and secure; and whether others will be there if they are in need. As they develop, children often generalize these attachment beliefs onto their relationship with others and ultimately to God and how His love will be appropriated.

It is at the core of this attachment bond formed between mother and child beginning in infancy where significant learning and emotional connection take place.

As a child moves through the developmental stages of life, various other players enter the stage. These include siblings, extended family, and, perhaps most importantly, peers. These relationships with significant others often confirm to the child the identity that has already been assigned to them through their family of origin. This is where any lies about their identity—who they are intrinsically—begin to become solidified, thus setting the stage for further destruction.

If God created us for relationship, it makes sense that our strongest emotional responses will be attached to our most intimate relationships. That's what fascinated Bowlby. He was interested in how children responded emotionally to prolonged separation from their parents. His research was conducted during an era where it was common to drop your child off at a hospital for surgery and leave them there for weeks at a time if necessary. The belief in those days was that caregivers were interchangeable, so a nurse could take care of a child as well as a mother could.

But Bowlby's observations of children in hospitals and

orphanages led him to argue strongly to the contrary. His research linked childhood mental health disorders to maternal deprivation and separation. He identified three phases a child would go through when separated from his or her mother: protest, despair, and detachment. When these states were prolonged, the child would simply detach. Children boxed up their needs for love and secure connection, and they put them on the shelf, sometimes leaving them there for decades.

Bowlby observed several responses from these so-called "orphaned" kids. After a few days of separation from their mom, some of the children responded with an attitude of "You know what? I don't need you." And when their mom came for a visit, they were more interested in the things she brought rather than being engaged with her. These children learned early on to wear a mask of self-sufficiency and independence, believing they alone could care for their own hearts.

Other children, the ones wired like Jesse, became more clingy and dependent. They would perform, please, and try harder and harder to get the love and connection they so desperately desired. They seemed to develop an internal working model that said "I'm not lovable, and others will abandon me because of my flaws." That meant they would have to try hard to be perfect so others wouldn't leave.[3]

Our attachment wounds

Let's be clear: Attachment wounds do not have to be centered on a traumatic event like abandonment. An attachment injury occurs when we experience the loss of secure connection, when we expect someone to be there for us and they aren't. When this happens repeatedly, a soul wound occurs. It could be a series of broken promises, a mostly absent parent, a sick parent, or an emotionally disconnected parent.

Jesse's mother was often emotionally unavailable. She would also try to manipulate her daughter into compliance by giving Jesse the cold shoulder when she voiced an opinion, didn't perform well, or became disagreeable. This created an attachment wound for Jesse. It also hindered her identity development. Jesse never learned to have or use her own voice because her fears of being rejected were so strong. She also formed a belief that she was never quite good enough for the love she craved.

Jesse's dad, on the other hand, would just get plain upset when she blew it. The result was that he would withhold affection and approval from her. He was rigid, controlling, and always had to be right. This left Jesse feeling *emotionally* abandoned. To cope with those feelings of rejection from her dad, she used the Pleaser and Try Harder masks.

When I showed Jesse the movie clip from *Hope Floats,* she wondered how it was relevant for her.

"My parents didn't get a divorce or abandon me," she said.

That was true. Jesse's attachment injuries were much more subtle then Bernice's, but nonetheless, they set the stage for a host of lies to develop in her young heart about her value and worth. Jesse did grow up feeling loved by her parents, and on the surface it all looked good. But deep inside she always felt like their love was predicated on her performance. Jesse felt like a lovely china doll that her mother wanted to dress up and show off. She was praised for her looks, her "good girl" personality, and doing well—period.

When I asked Jesse if she believed her parents accepted her, she said, "Not unless I'm perfect."

THE LIES WE BELIEVE

As we've seen, the lies we believe take root in our hearts from a very young age, and the enemy of our souls capitalizes on them. What do you think Satan spends most of his time on when it comes to a believer's life? Deception. That's what he did to Eve, that's what he did to my client Kim, and that's what he did to Jesse. Just like all of them, once we believe the lies, we're doomed because our actions follow our beliefs. If you don't know who you are, you'll base your identity on the externals: looks, weight, body image, success, or career.

So, what do we do about all these lies we believe, and is it possible that by believing them we can damage our brains? Absolutely. We'll learn more about that in chapter 5, but for now, let's take a look at how I helped Jesse see the truth.

The first thing I did was to teach her to notice and pay attention to the negative messages the Impostor tormented her with so that she could learn to refute them with the truth of God's Word. Here are some of the tapes that played in her head—see if any fit for you:

- You don't deserve to eat.
- You're fat and ugly.
- You're a disappointment.
- You'll never be good enough.
- You're inadequate.
- You have no value apart from your performance.
- You need to be invisible.
- You're such a failure.
- You can do better.
- You're a loser.
- You're not trying hard enough.
- You're too sensitive.
- No one will really love you unless you're thin.
- You'll be alone.

Next I helped her notice how all these negative accusations she constantly made against herself on a moment-by-moment basis were affecting her heart. I wrote down five of her core beliefs from the above list:

- I'm fat.

- I'm not good enough.

- I'm a failure.

- I have no value apart from my performance.

- Others will abandon me if I'm not perfect.

In one of our sessions I had Jesse read aloud all five of these beliefs over and over again for one minute straight. At the end of the minute I asked her how she felt about herself after repeatedly hearing those things. She said pretty lousy. I told her that's what she was doing every day, seven days a week, four weeks a month, twelve months a year. Three hundred sixty-five days of negative, defeating self-talk! No wonder she felt lousy about herself.

Negative self-talk serves to substantiate the lies we believe. It's like a dog constantly going back to its vomit. Self-talk appears on our radar screens all day long, sometimes even in telegraphic form. It can be something external that triggers us, like something someone says or something we see or hear in the outside world. The problem is we don't notice how negative self-talk affects our feelings and our mood because we're so used to saying this stuff to ourselves.

We're also reticent about giving up our negative self-talk because it's hard to convince ourselves of something we don't believe to be true. For example, Jesse believed she was fat, and no amount of my telling her differently would convince her. If she could see or pinch any skin off her stomach, that meant she was fat. She was strongly attached to that belief, so to help persuade her otherwise, I gave her some questions to ask herself so she could subject her negative self-talk to scrutiny. Here are a few of those questions:

- What evidence do I have to support this belief?

- Has this always been true?

- Am I being totally objective?

- What would an impartial observer say?

- What would I tell a friend who was struggling with this?

- What is the worst that could happen if I were (fill in the blank)?

- What could I do if the worst thing happened?

- How important will this be to me in the scheme of my life?

I told Jesse that even though negative self-talk was an ingrained habit, bad habits could be changed. Look around—every day, people quit smoking, drinking, and doing drugs. If your false beliefs won't stand up under careful examination, maybe you need to modify them.

This gives you plenty of room to develop your positive counter statements.

To begin, I gave her a few tips to actually construct the counter statements:

- Keep them in the present. "I know I feel fat now, but the truth is I am at a normal weight. My body is the temple of the Holy Spirit, and I need to honor God with my body."

- Use "I" statements. "I know I've gained some weight, but it's healthy for me. I have decided to focus on who I am inside and let that be what defines me."

- Have some degree of belief in their veracity. Don't write a counter statement if you really don't believe it. Try to modify false or irrational beliefs by challenging them and modifying them. Jesse couldn't say, "I'm not fat," but she could say, "Weighing more than I want to isn't the end of the world. I'm OK the way God made me." She was also able to reduce her anxiety by de-catastrophizing the irrational thought that she would die if she gained weight.

- Be positive. Instead of saying, "I'll fall apart if I gain weight; it will be the end of the world," Jesse learned to say, "If I gain a few pounds, I won't panic, and I won't die. No one has ever died from anxiety."

I told Jesse that the Impostor uses lots of different voices to get into her head. Here are a few we talked about:

- The Perfectionist
- The Judger
- The Critic
- The Victim

With each voice he assaulted her sense of identity. We've seen examples of the Perfectionist's voice, so let's take a look at what the other voices told her. The Judger was the voice of condemnation—another one of Satan's tactics. He constantly judged her performance, appearance, and body image. Nothing was ever good enough. The Critic followed up with what she did wrong, constantly pointing out her flaws and perceived imperfections. It was also the voice of comparison. She was never as good as…never did things right like…and didn't cut it. After a steady diet of this, Jesse would give up and become the victim, feeling helpless and losing heart: "I give up. I can't do this. I'm just a failure, and I'll never be able to overcome."

I told Jesse that every time she engaged in this negative self-talk, she was strengthening already established neural pathways in her brain. That got her attention. Here are a couple exercises I did with Jesse to show her how what she was telling herself affected her body, soul, and spirit.

I had Jess come up with five biblical counter statements that would refute each of the above lies she believed about herself. When she found herself engaging in negative self-talk, she was to counter that with a statement of truth. I had her do this every day for six weeks. I told her this would be important as we talked about her relationship with God.

Here are a couple statements she came up with that she really liked:

- "I am not a failure. I can overcome because I have the mind of Christ." (See 1 Corinthians 2:16.)

- "I'm not a loser. I am free from condemnation." (See Romans 8:1.)

- "I have the right to come boldly before the throne of grace to find mercy and grace in my time of need. I don't have to be perfect." (See Hebrews 4:16.)

- "I am not lacking anything because I have been made complete in Christ." (See Colossians 2:10.)

- "I should honor my body because I was bought with a price and I am not my own. I belong to Christ." (See 1 Corinthians 6:19–20.)

Here is another exercise I gave Jesse to do:

1. Sit in silence and solitude.

2. Notice each negative attribution you make against yourself.

3. When you hear the voice of condemnation from the Judge or Critic, attune yourself without judgment to God's heart toward you.

4. Use a verse of Scripture to focus on, and spend time meditating on that before God.

5. Ask the Father what He wants you to know about yourself. Each time you make a positive affirmation, you will be changing the neural networks that feed the Impostor. These old patterns are what enabled these negative attributions to become entrenched in your brain.

How Do You Cope?

By now you've seen that the coping strategies we use serve a threefold purpose:

- To help you get your needs met
- To avoid pain and rejection
- To solve your problems apart from God

Now it's time to take a look at how you've personally tried to manage and cope. Survey the following list and note the things you do to cope when the stresses of life weigh on you:

Become a people pleaser	Avoid conflict
Become a workaholic	Become a doormat
Stuff feelings or emotionally withdraw	Focus on appearance
Sleep, watch TV, or browse the Internet	Become critical
Judge or become critical of others	Hold a grudge
Caretake or try to fix or rescue others	Overeat
Become passive	Use food for comfort
Control	Become inhibited
Look to your appearance	Become self-deprecating
Stay busy	Become self-indulgent
Use substances to numb pain	Become self-sufficient
Become self-righteous	Become tense or nervous
Become pessimistic	Manipulate others
Become self-absorbed	Beat yourself up
Try hard	Become angry, hostile, and sarcastic
Perform for acceptance	Refuse to communicate
Become depressed	Look to relationships
Become obsessed with how you look	Engage in self-pity
Become aloof	Become the victim
Become bossy or demanding	Become jealous

Now that you've established some of your strategies for coping, you'll want to pay attention to how they fit into getting your needs met. Like Jesse, you'll need to practice the art of noticing. You may want to use a journal to record your insights. As you'll see, this art of noticing is the first step toward freedom—but hang on for more!

CONSIDER THIS

- Read Genesis 3:1–7. What lies has the enemy presented to you that you've bought into?

- Read 2 Corinthians 11:3. How have the lies caused you to be drawn away from the simplicity that is found in Christ?

- How have the lies affected your behavior?

- What have you looked to in order to gain a sense of adequacy?

- How is being known scary for you? Can you identify your fears?

- What will it take for you to risk coming out of hiding?

- Can you identify the strongest voices of your Impostor? Is it the Perfectionist, the Judge, or the Critic? Give some examples.

Chapter 4
THE SPINNING OF OUR SECRET SELF

Of what value is an idol carved by a craftsman? Or an image that teaches lies? For the one who makes it trusts in his own creation; he makes idols that cannot speak.

—HABAKKUK 2:18

IMAGINE FOR A moment a beautiful young woman. She sits staring in the mirror. Her face is young and full; her eyes are bright and alive. Maybe she's your daughter, wife, mother, or friend. In her right hand she holds a mask close to her face that bears her exact likeness. But looking closer, you can see there's something wrong. It's her eyes. They're a reflection of her heart—a window into the deepest places of her soul. She looks dead. Lost. Afraid. Alone. You have to look closely or you'll miss it, the sadness. It surrounds her like a dense fog, consuming who she really is.

She holds a heavy stone in her left hand. It's a reminder to her of the altar she's built for performance, pleasing, perfection, control, self-discipline, judgment, and condemnation. She is incapable of releasing it—at least for now. But there is hope, hope that one day she'll remove the mask and walk in the truth of who God's designed her to be.

The girl in the mirror is Jesse. But she could be anyone—a million other Jesses who have given themselves over to the voice of the Impostor to meet their needs for love, value, security, and acceptance. Some have chosen various substances; others, sex; and still others, food to numb the pain of loneliness and rejection.

The Unsuspecting Start

Jesse started out just wanting to lose a few pounds. As we've seen, she believed that in order to sustain the attention that was paid to her appearance, she needed to be perfect, look perfect, and perform perfectly. This fed her need for value and self-worth—at least on the surface. Looking back at her life, she began to see just how important that attention became, driving her to sacrifice herself on the altar of performance. Her entire life became centered on the belief that being thin and perfect would buy her the happiness and success she desperately craved. Those beliefs, fueled by the lies of the Impostor, nearly cost her life.

If we're honest, most of us can relate. We may not be starving ourselves to death in the search for significance, but we all use some type of performance strategy to get our needs met and manage our feelings of pain and rejection. Whether we're people pleasing, trying hard, avoiding confrontation, or not eating, we're sending a clear message that in order to be acceptable, we must hide our true selves.

The shame we feel about who we are leads us to create an Impostor—a false self to hide behind that helps protect our dreaded secret of being unmasked. Even those closest to us are not always privy to knowing our authentic self. If we can't convince ourselves of our own intrinsic worth, how in the world will others see us as valuable? The only solution is to pretend and continue to perform. Why? Because pretending provides the following perks:

- It helps us get our needs met for love, acceptance, value, security, and adequacy.

- It helps us avoid the pain and rejection of life.

- It helps us solve our problems independently from God.

- It gives us a false sense of meaning.

- It creates a false identity to avoid being known.

Perhaps the saddest thing about the Impostor is that we create it ourselves in response to the endless tapes playing in our heads that tell us we're falling short. Of course we don't realize all that at the beginning. We think we're the ones in control and calling all the shots. We're listening to his voice because we believe he can actually do something for us. The problem is that after a while, we can't tell who's who.

"IS THERE MORE TO ME?"

In her book *Life Without Ed*, Jenni Schaefer recounts how her therapist helped her notice the impact of her eating disorder identity by handing her a plastic Darth Vader mask to role-play his voice. In this way she learned to separate his identity from her own. Putting the mask on, she pretended to be Ed, and he said things like, "Jenni, you are fat. You will never recover. You will be miserable for the rest of your life." Taking off the mask, she learned to hear and respect her own voice and was able to counter his lies. She says this:

> Whenever I spoke in group, someone would ask, "Who is talking now? Is it Ed or Jenni?" I began to realize how frequently Ed expressed his opinion through my mouth. Sometime we would pull out the Darth Vader mask in order to help me make the split.[1]

Jenni didn't want to have her own voice in the beginning, as being thin meant too much to even consider change. But in time, as she was able to separate the eating disorder voice from her own, she realized there was a lot more to life than looking perfect. Jenni began to find significance in having her own identity and opinions.

That's what I tried to teach Jesse. Because she got the message that people paid attention to her because she was tiny and pretty, she didn't believe there was anything else about her worth noticing. So she never developed. She sat for decades as a small, frightened child with no identity outside of her appearance. I told her that once she developed a strong sense of self, rooted in who she is in Christ, the scales would begin to tip and she would like her voice better than the condemning voice of her Impostor. Her significance could then be grounded in something solid and not built on a lie.

The truth was, Jesse was tired of relentlessly running on the performance treadmill. She was tired of doing anything and everything to make sure she constructed a flawless life. I believe I got to the root of her fears during one of our sessions: Jesse was terrified of being alone. Because she had looked to everyone else to define her, she had no idea who she really was. To complicate matters, it was during this time when critical childhood development should have been occurring that the unspeakable was occurring instead.

"WHO AM I?"

Identity development is hard work. According to psychologist Erik Erikson, it requires that a child move through certain developmental stages and complete certain tasks. At each stage a psychosocial crisis arises and demands resolution. To successfully navigate through that developmental stage with a strong sense of self, we have to successfully negotiate the crisis. If we don't resolve the crisis, we move to the next developmental stage with a reduced ability to complete further stages, and therefore we display a more unhealthy sense of self.[2]

Part of Jesse's problem was she never really grew up.

She got stuck in the identity development stage instead of moving on to the role confusion stage of adolescence. In this adolescent stage a reexamination of identity takes place in order to answer the question "Who am I?"

As you've seen, Jesse had always been a people pleaser, conforming at the expense of being her own authentic self. While Jesse got plenty of affirmation from her parents and her peers because she was so pretty, that attention was misinterpreted.

The crisis for Jesse was to try to bring congruence to who she was apart from her looks and her performance. If you don't believe the externals are good enough, you listen to the Impostor to fill in the gaps. The key to finding your significance is to develop your authentic self, and you can't do that with two identities.

Jenni Schaefer says this:

> The ultimate goal is to disagree with and disobey Ed.
>
> As you practice separating from Ed, you will begin to make room for your own opinion—creating an opportunity for you to disagree with Ed. The thought of disagreeing may seem very scary and unrealistic to you. These responses are natural and understandable considering the power Ed has over your life. But as you continue to see yourself as *separate* from Ed, you will slowly learn to distinguish between what he is telling you and what you really think.[3]

Not even the approval of others seemed to satisfy the deep longing in Jesse's heart. It couldn't. Nothing could—except God, and Jesse wasn't ready to listen to Him, at least not yet. She always seemed to come up empty. Deep down inside she was afraid. Afraid of being unlovable. Afraid of being rejected. Afraid of making mistakes. Afraid of being alone.

Isn't that the deepest fear we all have—being unlovable and therefore alone? Even actress Demi Moore confessed to *Harper's Bazaar* magazine in 2012, "What scares me the most is that I'm going to ultimately find out at the end of my life that I'm really not lovable, that I'm not worthy of being loved. That there is something fundamentally wrong with me...and that I wasn't wanted here in the first place."[4]

Wow. Demi Moore seemed like she had it all. Great looks. Great body. Great career. Great life. Yet she confessed she was empty. She was afraid. She was insecure. Because it was all performance driven. It was counterfeit. It couldn't help but be. Her identity was birthed out of the voice of an Impostor telling her she wasn't good enough. Wasn't cutting it. She had to be young, hot, cool, and perfect to cut it in a town that's beauty and body image driven.

Somewhere along the line even G. I. Jane got tired of that workout regimen. She got scared, and when we get scared, we're vulnerable. We get real. We dig deep. We need. We become transparent. What was Demi's transparency about? Slowing down. Reflecting on a life lived. Wondering. Trying to find peace. Letting go. Not being the *best* anymore.

Think about how hard that must be. You were one of

the top movie stars in the country—and now someone else is a bigger deal. You're taking a back seat. Your time is waning. You love to act, and it's in your soul, but your glory is fading. Age catches up to women in Hollywood. It's someone else's turn now.

Whether you're a movie star, a sports icon, a supermodel, or anyone else who has ever loved a game, a ball, a set, a runway, or any career and watched it fade, well, let's just say the backside of glory can suck the life from your soul. It leaves you fearful of being left alone. There has to be something more.

James Masterson writes in *The Search for the Real Self*, "The false self plays its deceptive role, ostensibly protecting us—but doing so in a way that is programed to keep us fearful of being abandoned, losing support, not being able to cope on our own, not being able to *be* alone."[5]

Remember, children come into the world searching for significance. They are not born secure. If something happens to create fear in their hearts, an attachment injury or a trauma, fear becomes an all-powerful force capitalizing on that insecurity and sense of personal inadequacy. For a perfectionist like Jesse, any perceived failure dealt a deathblow to her sense of self. Her motivation to be perfect was an attempt to avoid the feelings that even a small failure engendered. This dramatically affected her ability to take risks or try something new. Because of that, her world became increasingly narrow, eventually causing her to slip into depression. By the time I saw her, she was so tired of trying to meet the impossible standards she set for herself, she had become hopeless.

The Impostor convinced Jesse she couldn't survive by herself because of her inadequacy. That made her more desperate for the approval of others and locked her into codependent ways of relating. On one hand, she was needy and clingy with others; on the other, she resented her dependence on them.

THE STRANGLEHOLD OF FEAR

Let's face it: We all fear something. God created us with a built-in alarm system to warn us of impending danger so that we can respond appropriately. There is such a thing as healthy fear. But when fear becomes debilitating, when we live with it every day and it cripples us, then something is terribly wrong.

Jesse didn't realize what she was experiencing was fear because the things that terrified her were the intangibles. Life without hiding meant she would be exposed, which would lead to rejection. Life without beauty meant she wouldn't be wanted. Life without being thin meant problems with being noticed. Life without a perfect performance meant she wouldn't measure up. Life that included risk meant stepping into the unknown and dealing with the unpredictable. All these thoughts paralyzed her.

Many of us are like Jesse in some way, scared without knowing why. We avoid confrontation, we say what everyone wants to hear, we chide ourselves for mistakes made, and we become peacemakers at any cost. Why?

Because we're afraid of what will happen if we take off our masks and let our true selves be exposed.

Here is where the Impostor takes front and center stage. Remember, he convinces us he has our best interests at heart—*that's the hook.* He assures us that if we keep pretending, we'll have nothing to fear. Yet by keeping our fears a secret, by not addressing them, we are only giving them room to grow. As they do, the truth becomes more and more distorted because fear blows our problems out of proportion. Perhaps most importantly, it distorts our concept of God. It makes us weak and causes us to believe in a small God.

The Book of Psalms is one of my favorite places to go in the Bible when I'm struggling with fear because King David doesn't mince words when he talks about his fears. Listen to his words in Psalm 55:4–5:

> My heart is in anguish within me; the terrors of death assail me. Fear and trembling have beset me; horror has overwhelmed me.

That's raw emotion. That's being willing to voice your pain. But where does David go with his fear? Look at verse 17: "Evening, morning and noon I cry out in distress, and he hears my voice." David knows he can run to his God because God is his secure base, his safe haven. He knows God will comfort him in times of duress—and that's what I wanted Jesse to know.

WHEN THE SECRETS START

Jesse built a counterfeit identity because the one she lived was far too painful. On the surface she had the perfect life, but that's because no one knew the truth. The core of her struggle wasn't the shame she felt about the eating disorder, or even falling short. It was what happened to her when she was little. She lived in a state of constant fear about the secret she could never tell. She finally began to trust me enough to share with me what happened.

Jesse was molested. The abuse started when she was about eight years old and continued for several years. She never wanted to say who the perpetrator was, but the trauma of those events changed the course of her entire life. She was too terrified and ashamed to tell anyone. So she hid it—for decades. Her heart lay frozen under layers and layers of unresolved hurt and pain.

Girls who have been sexually abused are extremely prone to eating disordered behavior. Mary Connors and Wanye Morse found that sexual abuse has been reported to occur in 30–65 percent of women with eating disorders.[6] A girl often turns to eating or starving in a subconscious attempt to reshape her body and express what has been done to her. If there is no space for the feelings associated with the abuse to be processed, if there is no room to regain and reclaim her sexual self, a girl will bury the intense feelings and rage caused by the trauma.

Once Jesse gave voice to the traumatic events of her life, the tide began to turn. At the time Jesse didn't know much about a personal relationship with God, but she assumed He wasn't good because of what He had allowed to happen to her.

But it would be that very pain that would eventually lead her straight into the Father's arms.

In the meantime, the Impostor helped Jesse feel good about herself—at least in the beginning. But as time went on, he filled her mind with shame-based lies that kept her imprisoned. The eating disorder was a way to cope and be in control when everything else was in chaos. It added an additional layer to the shame and self-loathing she felt, while at the same time empowering her by giving her control—or so she thought.

When Jesse performed well, the voice in her head would praise her. When she messed up, the Impostor reminded her she must do better the next time. He told her that as long as she was thin and beautiful and kept the dreaded secret, everything would be OK. But would it? Secrets rarely engender freedom.

Dr. Gura, in her book *Lying in Weight*, explains her secret struggle with anorexia. She tried to convince herself she was free, until one day she had a conversation with a friend that was pretty unsettling for her. Here's what she says:

> "I had an eating disorder, too," I said. "Anorexia."
>
> I used the "had" instead of "have" because, with years of therapy, I had recovered and gone on with life.
>
> And yet I wondered if it really was past, as Lauren asked me questions: How had my life

evolved as I approached 40? Did I still feel the need to control my eating? Did I like my body now?

At first, I answered in the detached way that I might talk about my grandmother's cataract operation. To me, battles with food belonged in the realm of adolescence, a sort of yellowed photo album that I, at 21, had set on the shelf.

Yet as I spoke about this thing that I had overcome, I knew that I was lying to myself. I did not feel liberated—not at all. It's more like this: I have a voice in my head that whispers like a ghost. It seduces. It tells me that no one will love me if I am fat. It says that what I do is never enough. It promises that if I follow its rules, skipping meals, swimming extra laps, not eating this or that, avoiding meat and chicken and fish and dairy products, I will be safe. But most of the time I do not feel safe—just closed up and isolated.

I have tried to ignore the voice. When I scream, "Leave me alone! Let me enjoy life without these crazy rules!" it snickers and goes into hiding. Then there is silence, and for a time, even for years, I am free.

Or so I think.[7]

Secrets take a lot of energy to uphold. The fear that someone will find us out must be prevented at all costs. So we hide—from everyone. This life of secrecy is profoundly isolating. As Gura points out some twenty-five years post-recovery, she finds she still lives in isolation.

For Jesse, the cost of maintaining the secret of her trauma and her eating disorder was high. It affected every aspect of her life: the quality of her relationships, her mood, social life, family life, and work life, not to mention her mental health and well-being. The question I continued to ask her to consider was "Is it worth it?"

There was only one place Jesse would ever find the unconditional love and acceptance her heart longed for. It was in the arms of God. That would require risk. That would require evaluating what Jesse believed about God. She was scared, but she was willing to go there with me. Are you?

CONSIDER THIS

- What secrets have kept you in bondage?

- Is there shame somewhere in your past or present that's causing you to hide? If so, how are you hiding?

- What would you name as your three greatest fears?

- What outcomes do you predict in light of these fears?

- How have you dealt with your fears?

- Is there any abuse in your past? If so, have you told your story to someone safe? If you haven't told anyone, what might be hindering you?

- Have you ever felt that to be acceptable, you must hide your true self? How have you hidden?

Chapter 5
YOUR BRAIN ON GOD

If you contemplate God long enough, some-
thing surprising happens in the brain.[1]
—ANDREW NEWBERG, MD

COUNSELORS HAVE AT their disposal a lot of great treatment modalities to help clients deal with a whole host of mental health disorders. Many of them are highly effective and have been empirically validated over years of testing and trial. But what if there was something more we could teach people? What if we could take some of what we've learned from attachment theory and from neuroscience about the brain and how it wires itself in response to love and secure connection and assist folks in making sense of their life schemata? What if it could allow them to feel and experience being known at the heart level? What if we could help them rewire neural pathways and give them a deep sense of feeling known by the God who created them?

The good news is we can! Because of what we've learned about the brain and its neuroplasticity (a fancy word for the brain's ability to restructure itself), we now know we can reshape neural networks and reprogram maladaptive ways of thinking and relating.

While all our theories of counseling are helpful and a necessary part of the healing process, I've found that real healing comes by laying a foundation for people to know, understand, and experience the love of their heavenly Father. When identity can be rooted in the truth of who we are in Christ, we stand on solid, immovable ground.

To begin that process with Jesse, I had to first explore her currently held beliefs about God.

WHAT DO YOU THINK ABOUT GOD—REALLY?

Most Americans say they're Christians, but most don't believe in a loving God who cares about their hearts:

> According to a new book called *America's Four Gods* by Paul Froese and Christopher Bader, the way Americans view God falls into four categories.
>
> Froese and Bader, both professors at Baylor University, used polling data from a 2008 survey to break down how Americans believe in God.
>
> The survey showed that about 28 percent of Americans believe in an "authoritative God."
>
> "Someone who has an authoritative God believes in a God that is very judgmental and very engaged in the world at the same time," said Bader, adding that they also tend to be evangelical and male.
>
> For 22 percent of Americans, mostly evangelical women, they characterize the almighty as a "benevolent God" who is thoroughly involved in their lives but is loving, not stern.[2]

Somewhere along the line, we have all decided some things about God—things that affect how we perceive

Him and how we receive from Him. This is really the heart of attachment. Is God a secure base and safe haven? Does He care about our hearts? Is He really attuned to us? And will He be there for us if we need Him?

As we grow up, we begin to learn some things about God from our parents. When we discover He is the ultimate authority figure, we base our impressions of Him on the thoughts, feelings, and experiences we've had with our earthly parents. If our parents were critical, demanding, unloving, or abusive, then how might we come to view God? Not in a very good light, I'm afraid. And yet this is exactly what happens—we take all the conditions of worth that were imposed upon us as kids by our parents, and we generalize all those impressions onto our relationship with God. In other words, we come to believe God is just like our parents.

Remember, we come into this world asking those fundamental questions: "Who am I? Am I loved? Am I valued? Will my attachment figure be there for me when I need comfort?" As we get older and we're trying to make sense of life and the world around us, we begin asking the question "Who is God?" If we grow up to believe we can't trust the heart of God, given the life messages we've received—if we believe God is unloving, uncaring, distant, or detached—removing the masks we wear in the name of protecting ourselves from pain will be difficult. If we've never developed an ability to comprehend our own internal world, if we've never experienced relationships that were safe and secure, if we've never learned to be attuned to the emotional states of others, it will be harder for us to connect to God's love.

The truth is, what we believe about God will determine how we order everything else in our lives—and in our brains.

GOD-WIRED

Dr. Andrew Newberg, author of *How God Changes Your Brain*, is a neuroscientist at the University of Pennsylvania. He has studied the brains of religious people for the last decade. His findings validate the already established oceans of scientific research that suggest a belief in a loving God and the use of spiritual practices like meditation and contemplative prayer actually stimulate our brains and helps them grow and heal.

Dr. Newberg found that "in Judeo-Christian prayer, the frontal lobe activates just as it would in normal conversation. To the brain, talking to God is indistinguishable from talking to a person."[3] That makes sense, considering the Judeo-Christian tenet that God is a personable, communicating being. And for Christians, He *is* a person, Jesus Christ. People with these faith backgrounds are talking to a real Person when they pray.

For people from other religious backgrounds, Newberg found their brains did not activate in the same way. Their practice is not toward "a person who can be directly spoken to but rather an essence that can be visualized during deep meditation."[4] And when atheists were asked to meditate, their brains were not active at all because to them, "God is unimaginable."[5]

Dr. Newberg concludes that all religions create neurological experiences and that while God is unimaginable for atheists, for religious people God is as real as the physical world.[6]

Neuroscientist Richard Davidson says you can change your brain with experience and training. "You can sculpt your brain just as you'd sculpt your muscles if you went to the gym," he says. "Our brains are continuously being sculpted, whether you like it or not, wittingly or unwittingly."[7] This is called neuroplasticity.

How does this apply to beliefs about a punitive, distant, or uncaring God? It activates the brain's fear circuits and your body's stress responses. It results in greater inflammatory problems as well. For someone like Jesse, who believed God was responsible for her abuse, even though it wasn't true, it changed her brain. She couldn't access the God of love because someone who was supposed to love her had betrayed her, so she saw God through that lens. What followed was a core fear that implanted itself in her heart and threatened to overtake her life.

BRAIN NEUROBIOLOGY 101

Each of us can probably identify one, or more, monumental and intensely personal experience that changed our lives and radically impacted our belief system. For Jesse, the first one came when she was eight. She had no context for the trauma of her abuse because when we're that young, we are extremely egocentric in our thinking. We also lack the ability to think abstractly. Jesse came to believe the abuse she suffered was somehow her fault. The result was a deep sense of shame that followed as she grew up.

As she sat in my office recounting the story, I could see the impact it had on her. The abuse was one of those experiential moments that helped set up and solidify an internal working model of herself and of God. It also changed the neurocircuitry in her brain. As Jesse grew up, she began to question how a loving God could have allowed such a horrible thing to happen to her. Her feelings told her God wasn't good. Together we would try to make sense of the unspeakable.

But how do our thoughts, feelings, and beliefs about God actually impact the physical function of our brain? Before we jump into that, let's do a short lesson in brain science. Get two almonds and two walnuts, and put them in one hand, making a fist around them with your thumb tucked under your other fingers. Bend your arm. You're now looking at a visual representation of your brain. The two almonds in your hand represent your amygdala, the place in your limbic system that gives you a "danger, danger" signal (fight or flight). The two walnuts are your thalamus, which sends sensory information to all other parts of your brain.[8]

Your forearm is your spinal cord, coming up through to the wrist. Coming into the skull is the brainstem and the limbic areas, which regulate emotions and arousal; they are below the cortex. The cortex is your knuckles.

The flat part of your fingers is the part of the brain behind your forehead that regulates the subcortical limbic and brainstem areas.[9]

To really understand how the brain operates, let's look at a practical example of how this might play out in your everyday life. Let's say I invite you over to my house to go swimming in my pool. You know I have a lot of landscaping in my backyard, and I've told you that on occasion we've had snakes out there. You come over for a swim, and as you're walking over to jump in the pool, you notice something long and black moving in the grass.

You start to freak out. Your heart rate goes through the roof, your blood pressure goes up, and you start breathing rapidly. The alarm system in your brain (the amygdala) sends out the "danger, danger" signal to your adrenal glands to let you know there is trouble. Snake! Your adrenals release the stress hormones of cortisol and adrenaline. The alarm also sends a 911 call to your brain's operation center (hypothalamus), which sends out hormones that release signals to your pituitary gland. All this causes a further increase in the stress response.

You are now primed to respond to danger. Blood flow decreases in your internal organs and is sent to your muscles. Glucose is dumped into your bloodstream, and respiration increases. You take off running like greased lightning to get away from the snake. Your prefrontal cortex, the information processing center of your brain where reasoning and thinking take place, is finally activated, and you are able to look rationally at the black *rubber* snake I threw into the grass to fool you!

With this simple illustration it's easy to see how what we believe holds tremendous power over us—and our brain. Our beliefs are the most powerful things we chose because our beliefs affect our thoughts, and our thoughts affect what happens in our neural networks.

What does all this have to do with an intimate relationship with God? Glad you asked.

In my counseling practice I often do a simple exercise with my clients to assess their concept of God. I have them draw a picture of their relationship with God on a *feelings* level—no words. The results are very telling, but the point is this: I'm getting them to *think* about God, and just the mention of Him stimulates activity in different parts of their brain. That's important because when we talk about contemplation and meditation practices—spiritual disciplines—later, we'll see exactly which parts of the brain are responsible for the rewiring process that can occur as we connect to the real God of the Bible, not the imagined mean guy in the sky.

Here's the skinny on what each part of the brain we're interested in does when we think about God:

The frontal cortex of the brain is responsible for thinking and reasoning, so this area creates all your thoughts about who God is and tries to answer all those "why" questions you have about His nature and character. Remember the two walnuts you put in your hand? They represent the thalamus, that part of the brain that gives meaning to your concept of God. It's responsible for processing information and sending it out to the rest of your brain.

The amygdala is the emotional center of the brain. When overstimulated, it causes you to respond on a feelings level to your beliefs about God. If you believe God is harsh, punitive, or authoritarian, it will most likely evoke a fear response; whereas if you believe in a loving God, you will most likely experience peace and calm, thanks to an area responsible for suppressing activity in the amygdala called the anterior cingulate.

If beliefs of God evoke fear or punishment, they can quite literally damage parts of your brain.[10] I have had many clients who have had obsessive-compulsive thoughts about God's wrath; they constantly worry about being punished because they were somehow bad. They ruminate about losing their salvation, or they question if they are really saved in the first place.

Religions that propagate a God who is waiting to punish us for the slightest infraction incite fear, and the fear response activates the amygdala. When a fear response becomes chronic, the over-activated amygdala sends out macrophages (special white blood cells), which begin to send out inflammatory cytokines to help defend us. The problem is, these inflammatory factors can cause damage to all types of neurons in our bodies, including our insulin receptors, making it harder for the body to use glucose. Prolonged activation of the stress cascade increases the risk of type 2 diabetes, obesity, high cholesterol, heart attack, stroke, ulcers, and inflammatory diseases.[11] Over time it can get really ugly.

Dr. Newberg's findings suggest that belief in a loving God, along with prayer and meditation practices, are beneficial to your emotional and physical health and well-being. Furthermore, his research supports several fundamental neurological truths:

- Your thoughts clearly affect the neurological functioning of your body.

- Optimism is essential for a healthy brain.

- Positive thoughts neurologically suppress negative thoughts.

- When you change the way you think, you begin to change your outward circumstances.

- Consciousness, reality, your mind, and your spiritual beliefs are profoundly interconnected and inseparable from the functioning of your brain.[12]

If our thoughts affect the neurological functioning of our bodies, then it makes sense that we need to be watching what we tell ourselves, especially about God.

THE POWER OF COGNITIVE DISTORTIONS

One of Jesse's biggest problems was the cognitive distortions she had developed over the years, based on her experiences. My first goal was to educate her on some of the most common thinking errors and have her burn those into her brain cells. Jesse had to notice what she was doing before she could change it. The problem with negative self-talk is that doing it becomes so natural for us that we don't even recognize it. Most people aren't aware of what cognitive distortions are, so here are a few I went over with Jesse as they related to her concept of God.

All-or-nothing thinking

People like Jesse think in extremes. They think in terms of "all or nothing" with regard to just about anything that concerns them. All-or-nothing thinking means you see things as black or white, no shades of gray and no middle ground.

Jesse would say, "God must hate me."

"Hate is a pretty strong word," I'd say. "What makes you think that?"

"He let me be abused and did nothing—how about that!" she would fire back.

"I understand," I'd say. "But if God is love, He isn't capable of hating anyone. The only thing He hates is evil. What was done to you was evil. Could you try and modify that belief?"

"OK, maybe He does love me," she'd say, "but He has a funny way of showing it."

The idea for overcoming all-or-nothing thinking is to bring your thoughts into middle ground, whether they have to do with your weight, your body image, or your concept of God. I had Jesse look up several scriptures about God's love. I asked her to ponder those as she considered her irrational beliefs. Now that she had a verse of Scripture to use as a plumb line for truth, she could construct a counter statement of truth whenever she started thinking God hated her. Here's what we came up with for her to tell herself:

- "God so loved Jesse that He gave his one and only Son so that she might have eternal life."
- "Even though I feel like God hated me, the truth is that He loves me immeasurably more than I can ask or imagine."

Now she had something to tell herself—truth—that would help to rewire her neural pathways.

Catastrophizing

People who struggle with anxiety are especially prone to catastrophizing. They focus their attention on the worst possible outcomes in any given situation. It doesn't matter how irrational their thoughts may seem; they worry and ruminate that they most certainly will occur. Catastrophizing is rooted and sustained through fear. Most of the time those fears are an unrealistic overestimation of a threatening event occurring and an underestimation of our ability to deal adaptively with it.

Jesse worried about God punishing her because she was bad. She was always waiting for the shoe to drop. The Impostor convinced her to lie about her eating disorder all the time, so the voice inside her head told her God was sorely displeased with her and would surely send her to hell. She felt powerless to deal with that.

Jesse also worried God hated her because she doubted Him. Because Jesse was a people pleaser, she felt she could never question God. She was afraid to ask the million questions that plagued her heart about Him. This shut down activity in her prefrontal cortex. When she thought about eternity, she would get visibly upset. She had recurring nightmares of hell and damnation and saw herself shut off from all mankind. These thoughts were activating the fear response in her amygdala. It's no wonder she didn't want to talk about God! It was better to bottle it all up and deny there was a problem.

The key to freedom for Jesse lay in her willingness to go to these places of fear and not avoid them. I assured her that although she would experience unpleasant feelings, she wouldn't die from facing these fears. I told her God was a benevolent Father, waiting to take her into His loving arms and provide comfort for her. Furthermore, anyone who thought God was like she imagined would be prone to those kinds of thoughts and fears, and while those thoughts and fears may create anxiety for a short period of time, the catastrophic outcome she imagined would not occur.

Jesse never saw herself as strong. Her constant worrying sidetracked her from tapping into her capacity to cope with even the smallest disaster. Therefore she continually sold herself short when it came to her ability to cope. But Jesse was really remarkably resilient. I told her that people not only survive bad things happening, but also they can actually grow and thrive in spite of them with God's help.

Jumping to conclusions/mind reading

Jumping to conclusions is something all of us do, especially with those we're closest to. Jesse did this a lot. She concluded that because she didn't feel God's love, she must not have it. She concluded that because God didn't stop her abuse, He didn't love her. She concluded that because she had an eating disorder, God was punishing her. Jesse had no evidence to support any of these beliefs. Jumping to conclusions/mind reading generally finds us believing the worst-case scenarios. So before you go there, catch yourself, and ask the following questions:

- What evidence do I have to support this belief?

- Could there be an alternative explanation for this?

- Do I have any evidence to support an alternative?

- How beneficial is this line of thinking for me?

Emotional reasoning

The beliefs many of us currently hold about God generally rest on our feelings about Him. How accurate is a concept of God based on what we think or feel? Not very accurate. In fact, what we think or feel about God often has little to do with the truth. Furthermore, our feelings aren't always a good indicator that God's life is even in us.

How do we turn our feelings into facts? Through the

cognitive distortion of emotional reasoning. This is a powerful thinking error because it can assault our sense of intrinsic worth. Jesse *felt* unlovable. She made that into a fact by believing she *was* unlovable. She then *acted* out of that belief by wearing all kinds of masks to make her more lovable.

The same holds true for our thoughts about God. If we *feel* He is unjust or unloving because of what we've heard growing up or what we've experienced, we make that into a fact and believe He *is* unjust and unloving.

You see, our feelings are not necessarily bearers of truth; they are just instantaneous internal responses to the external events of everyday life. They aren't moral or immoral, good or bad, right or wrong. They just are what they are.

As we've seen, our thoughts hold the power to heal or to destroy. Every day we have hundreds of them coming into our minds, many of which are colored by these cognitive distortions we all tend to make. Only the thoughts we accept as true and place our confidence in become our beliefs. That's important because, as we noted earlier, our actions will always follow our beliefs. If we fill our heads with enough lies about our intrinsic worth, in time we'll begin to feel, believe, and act as if we have no self-worth. We will allow our feelings to dictate our reality instead of letting God's Word determine it.

When we make our feelings bearers of truth, we are walking on shifting sand. Jesse had no plumb line to measure truth because she didn't know the truth about herself or about God. The God she believed in was not the God I tried to teach her about. Scripture says, "You will know the truth, and the truth will set you free" (John 8:32). So to know truth, we have to store the truth in our hearts. That means we have to have an intellectual knowledge of God through the reading of His Word. There we learn who He is. We can see His heart, and we can draw conclusions about His goodness.

Negative self-talk

Negative self-talk is subtle. How many times a day do you call yourself stupid, fat, worthless, or some other derogatory name? Do you have any idea what a steady diet of that is doing to your brain? If you did the exercises in chapter 3, you were able to experience on a feelings level what it's like to put yourself down all the time. It may seem funny, but it's no joke to your neural pathways. With each negative attribution you make, you're strengthening those old pathways; Donald Hebb pointed out as early as 1949, "Neurons that fire together wire together."[13]

To help Jesse know the truth about God, I reviewed her concept of Him, looking for false beliefs. I helped her replace the lies she believed with solid scriptural truths. I taught her how to use the spiritual disciplines (more on that later) to connect to the heart of God. I taught her truth about her heavenly Father and showed her how to practice the presence of God, and He showed up and did the rest. This intimate experiential knowing of God helped Jesse restore her relationship with Him.

I helped Jesse see her identity in Christ by getting her to trust me enough to remove the masks the Impostor convinced her she needed to wear. She was wounded in the context of relationship, but she also found healing in the context of relationship—first with me, then with God.

WHAT ELSE SHAPES THE BRAIN?

Dr. Dan Siegel, in his groundbreaking work *The Developing Mind,* proposes that the mind develops at the interface of neurophysiological processes and interpersonal relationships. Here's the lowdown on how interpersonal relationships affect the brain and how it organizes itself around them:

> Relationship experiences have a dominant influence on the brain because the circuits responsible for social perception are the same as or tightly linked to those that integrate the important functions controlling the creating of meaning, the regulation of bodily states, the modulation of emotion, the organization of memory, and the capacity for interpersonal communication. Interpersonal experience thus plays a special organizing role in life and the ongoing emergence of brain function throughout the lifespan.[14]

If God is relational in His orientation, it makes sense that He created us for relationships and that those relationships would have a powerful effect on us. Who are the significant others who contribute to shaping and wiring our brains? Here are a few:

- Church

- Peers

- Life circumstances

Unfortunately the church can be notorious for shooting its own wounded. Church is supposed to be safe, a place where we feel we can come to share the wounding of our hearts. However, it often becomes a place of judgment and condemnation if we don't fit into the status quo. The widespread abuse from clergy and pastors has done much to destroy people's concept of God. Sadly, many of my clients have been deeply wounded by church members, legalism, and not-so-Christlike love.

When we step outside of the confines of the home and begin to relate in the world around us, peers enter the picture. They help to either confirm or deny the already established messages we have begun to form about ourselves and the world around us. For Jesse, her peers were usually jealous of her because she was so pretty, but because she had a pleaser personality, she did make a lot of friends, including several who stood by her through the thick and the thin.

Life circumstances are probably the strongest force in shaping our concept of God. If our lives have been relatively easy, without too many trials, it's easy to believe God is good. If, however, life has been difficult, traumatic, or full of negative events, believing in God's goodness becomes a lot more difficult.

In the movie *Bruce Almighty* we get a clear picture of

how life circumstances can color our view of God. Jim Carrey plays Bruce Nolan, a television reporter who is passed over for promotion in favor of his rival. He becomes furious, and his anger gets him suspended from the station. What follows is a series of unfortunate events, and Bruce decides that God is out to get him. He says, "God is just a mean kid sitting on an anthill with a magnifying glass, and I'm the ant. He could fix my life in five minutes if He wanted to, but He'd rather burn off my feelers and watch me squirm."[15]

Bruce based his concept of God on how well life was going. If circumstances were good, God was OK. If they weren't, God was just a mean guy in the sky trying to hammer him. Funny movie, but as we've seen, this is exactly how many people view God. They base their beliefs about who He is on what they believe He has allowed into their lives.

Whether life has been positive or negative, we still need a secure base and a safe haven to cling to. What does it mean to have God as a secure base? It means that in times of trouble, we can run to Him. It means that when we close our eyes at night, when we cry out in the depths of despair, who do we really believe is there? Can God provide us with a sense of felt security? Is He near? Will He come through for us when we need Him?

Jesse's deep sense of insecurity and her search for significance made her most willing to move toward God. She desperately needed to believe He was safe as we processed the trauma of her losses.

CONSIDER THIS

- What is your concept of God?

- How was it shaped, and by whom was it shaped—parents, peers, church, other authority figures?

- Do you see God as good?

- Is God good even when the bottom drops out of your life? How so?

- What have you done or what are you currently doing to know God more intimately?

- Do you see God as distant, unloving, or performance-based?

- How would you characterize your relationship with God at this time?

- How ready are you to have deeper intimacy with God?

Chapter 6
OUR UNATTENDED SORROWS

My eye is wasted away from grief, my soul and my body also.
For my life is spent with sorrow and my years with sighing.
—PSALM 31:9–10

LOSSES COME IN all shapes and sizes, but none has a more powerful impact on the human soul than the loss of innocence. Jesse was robbed of her childhood, and the effects of her abuse had far-reaching implications on her life trajectory and her heart. Her inability to touch the wounded places of her soul left her sorrow unattended.

Looking through the lens of loss, everything we believe comes into question. We doubt others, God, and ourselves. We feel dismantled, as if a part of us is missing. The road back can be long and painful. When those we're supposed to trust betray us in the most vile and unimaginable ways, we emerge as a shadow of our former self.

Perhaps the hardest part for Jesse was suffering alone. Pain is a personal, private, and messy business, but if we can take a risk and allow another to walk alongside us and become our tutor, in time we can learn from our sorrows and move forward. But in order to learn, we have to break the silence. We have to connect with the pain, and we have to put words to what was unspeakable.

That's where Jesse and I began her grief work. I had her make a list of all the relational and the abstract losses in her life. Relational losses include such things as death, divorce, and betrayal. Abstract losses are less discernable, sometimes hidden from our own conscious awareness. They would include things such as:

Shattered dreams	Loss of passion
Role loss	Unmet expectations
Loss of health	Loss of innocence
Loss of identity	Loss of childhood
Loss of appearance	Loss of hope
Loss of freedom	Unfulfilled goals or desires
Loss of feeling known	Loss of trust
Loss of relationship	Loss of career

The importance of noticing the effects of these losses on our hearts is critical because the long-range impact of unresolved grief will gradually shut down our hearts. Stephen Levine says this in his book *Unattended Sorrow:*

> Spanning these long-unattended sorrows, which gradually closes us down, are the slowly accumulating burden of disappointment and disillusionment, the loss of trust and confidence that follows the increasingly less satisfactory arch of our lives— until finally, at the far end of the spectrum we're so mired in lost hope that we are barely able to find ourselves.[1]

What greater travesty can there be than realizing at the end of our lives that we have not known our true self? When we don't know who we are, we look to something else to fill us. It's usually some sort of addictive behavior to numb the pain of feeling lost. Jesse's drug of choice revolved around restricting food, but others have chosen alcohol, drugs, self-harm, pornography, or a host of other addictions in the search for their identity. They always come up empty.

Noticing our losses requires time, attention, and work. Neglected sorrow doesn't just include what we had and lost; it also includes all the things we wanted or expected that *didn't* happen in our lives. It doesn't have to be big things; it can be a collection of small, seemingly insignificant things that pile up.

My friend Jack's whole life was impacted by the business decisions he made that didn't turn out the way he had hoped. He never saw those events as losses until we talked about how they affected him. Company setbacks along with the market forces cost him a big promotion he deserved. When what he had worked so hard for didn't happen, he became embittered and began to drink to numb his pain. He began to question everything, especially his ability to make decisions. He also questioned his leadership skills. This paralyzed him.

Jack had never processed how the loss of his promotion had affected his heart. He never realized how it had affected his belief system about his own capabilities and about the world around him. But once he did begin to process these things, he was able to regain his footing.

The smaller losses in life need our attention just as much as the big ones. The sadness they create must be tended to because it connects you to what you had hoped for but lost and who you became in the process.

Unattended sorrow can be a lot like walking around with a low-grade fever and never really noticing you're sick. It lingers in your soul until the pain begins to feel normal. As time passes, you may notice that you trust the world a little bit less, but you don't really know why. You hold others on the periphery of your life because you don't know how to invite them in closer. You feel dead inside. You feel empty, so you hide, and you create an Impostor to help you cope.

Unfortunately, you can't fool your brain.

The story of unattended sorrows is encoded in your brain just as it's written on the tablet of your heart. Left unchecked, the brain literally stays frozen. The trouble is we construct walls around our hearts to tell our brain we're OK. The evidence overwhelmingly speaks to the contrary, however, and is revealed in the bruised places your brain recognizes as trauma. Trauma sand-blasts the brain to its core, and Jesse's brain was trauma-tized. Memories of trauma are encoded and stored in the brain's limbic area; therefore, behavior and memory can't be changed simply by talk therapy or changing one's thought patterns. More is required.

The story of trauma can be revealed through the body and the sensations it experienced through the events that occurred. These must not be ignored in the therapeutic process. In his book *In an Unspoken Voice* Dr. Peter Levine says:

Therapeutic approaches that neglect the body, focusing mainly on thoughts (top-down processing), will consequently be limited. I propose instead that, in the initial stages of restorative work, bottom-up processing needs to be standard operating procedure. In other words, addressing a client's "bodyspeak" first and then, gradually, enlisting his or her emotion, perception and cognition is not merely valuable, it's essential. The talking cure for trauma survivors should give way to the unspoken voice of the silent but strikingly powerful, bodily expressions as they surface to "sound off" on behalf of the wisdom of the deeper self.[2]

Trauma demands one put words to what seems impossible to speak. When words won't come, the body communicates though things like shaking, shouting, thrashing, catatonia, dissociation, hyperarousal, rage, anxiety, muscle tremors, sweating, difficulty breathing, nausea, chest pain, increased startle response, pacing, or rocking motions. All these symptoms suggest the body is responding to the aftershocks of the traumatic event. These symptoms may last weeks, months, or years, depending on the severity of the trauma and if it is treated.

Jesse was traumatized by her sexual abuse, and because of that she stayed frozen. Like Jenny Lauren, she couldn't complete the developmental tasks necessary to move forward in her life. Thus, she always felt helpless. She believed there was nothing she could do about what happened to her, so why talk about it? Why bother with it? She was a victim of life and circumstance.

She didn't realize it for a long time, but she was raging inside.

ANGER

Anger turned inward makes the soul sick. It's a result of unattended sorrow. Anger sits on top of more vulnerable emotions, guarding our hearts from things like sadness, hurt, rejection, and fear. It protects us from getting hurt again—or so we believe. It's so much easier to be mad than to risk opening the floodgates of unattended sorrow. We fear that if we do that, we will never recover, so we allow the anger to sit and fester, growing deep roots of bitterness in our souls.

We don't talk about it. We don't allow ourselves to feel it. And we don't want to let go of it because if we do, we'll have to figure out some other way to live. That's much too scary for many of us.

To heal, we have to recognize that our anger is our responsibility and deal with it. No one else is going to do this difficult work for us. The solution for anger is to forgive, and we can't even consider that as an option when we've been physically or emotionally abused.

With her "hold it all together" demeanor, no one would have guessed Jesse was so angry or so disconnected from herself. She didn't even realize it until her mother died. Then something snapped. It was unexplainable. Jesse's eating disorder became so bad, she had to be hospitalized. What was happening was her heart was being re-traumatized. It brought all the rage she carried on the inside to the surface, demanding attention. Remember, threat or danger signal the normal fight-or-flight response in our limbic brain. This motivates us to action—to fight or flee. When the ability to fight or flee is thwarted, the brain can automatically default to freeze. Immobilization can lead to a sense of overwhelming helplessness and terror. Levine explains:

> Just as the immobilized animal (in the presence of a predator) comes out ready for violent counterattack, so too does a traumatized person abruptly swing from paralysis and shutdown to hyper-agitation and rage. Fear of this rage and the associated hyper intense sensations prevents a tolerable exit form immobility unless there is education, preparation, titration and guidance. The fear of rage is also the fear of violence—both toward others and against oneself. The exiting of immobility is inhibited by the following double bind: to come back to life, one must feel the sensations of rage and intense energy. However, at the same time, these sensations evoke the possibility of mortal harm. This possibility inhibits sustained contact with the very sensations that bring relief from the experience of immobility, thereby leading to resolution.[3]

To heal, Levine suggests a person be gradually led into and out of the immobility sensations many times, each time returning to a calming state of balance. Balance is achieved by creating a safe place in the person's mind to go to when they become overwhelmed by memories of the trauma. Then, slowly, fear and helplessness can be separated from the inability to escape from the trauma (the immobility response). According to Levine, this allows the "unwinding" of the fear and freeze to begin.[4]

Once the unwinding occurs, we can begin to tap into the anger that lies buried within the soul. Anger is a normal response to pain, trauma, or a blocked goal. Jesse was angry with herself, angry with others, and angry with God. Her anger, however, became buried beneath the conscious surface in an attempt to protect herself from reexperiencing the paralysis and helplessness of her trauma. Avoidance only serves to prolong the inevitable and often makes the encounter with immobility even more terrifying. For empowerment to occur, we must be allowed to restore an active defense system.

To begin that process, I encouraged Jesse to do deal with the anger she had toward her mother for not protecting her. We began by making a list of each event where she had experienced feeling defenseless. Jesse listed several things she had experienced with her mother:

- She didn't listen when I finally tried to tell her what happened.

- She knew I was anxious a lot and did nothing.

- She didn't protect me from my dad's angry outbursts.

- She cared more about my appearance than who I was.

- She never stood up for me.

Next, we listed each belief Jesse held about herself because of her mother's perceived inability to give her what she needed. She came up with things like:

- I wasn't worth protecting.

- I wasn't valuable.

- I wasn't worth the risk for her to overcome her own demons to be there for me.

Then we recorded what Jesse had hoped for or expected that she didn't get. These were the unattended sorrows she was finally able to put into words—things like:

- I had expected to be nurtured.

- I had hoped to be cherished for who I was, not how I looked.

- I needed to be protected and to feel secure.

- I needed to be heard.

After we completed the list on her mom, I encouraged Jesse to do battle with God—to give voice to her rage at Him for allowing what happened. We searched the Scriptures to put words to her pain. I gave her the following verses:

Why, LORD, do you stand far off? Why do you hide yourself in times of trouble?

—PSALM 10:1

How long, LORD? Will you forget me forever? How long will you hide your face from me? How long must I wrestle with my thoughts, and day after day have sorrow in my heart? How long will my enemy triumph over me?

—PSALM 13:1–2

My God, my God, why have you forsaken me? Why are you so far from saving me, so far from my cries of anguish? My God, I cry out by day, but you do not answer, by night, but I find no rest.

—PSALM 22:1–2

I say to God my Rock, "Why have you forgotten me? Why must I go about mourning, oppressed by the enemy?" My bones suffer mortal agony as my foes taunt me, saying to me all day long, "Where is your God?"

—PSALM 42:9–10

Jesse felt forgotten by God. This created a huge void in her soul. If God didn't think she was worth protecting, what did she have left?

She had started to read her Bible and meditate on some verses, sitting with them at my request for several days. Slowly something started to happen in her heart. God was dismantling the walls, brick by brick, until one day she had a major breakthrough. Jesse heard God speak to her through one of the verses she was studying. She no longer wanted the enemy of her soul to have victory over her life. She was tired of fighting the wrong battle.

Jesse's anger at God didn't go away in some magical moment, but she was now able to see Him as a friend. She was able to tell Him about her anger and the hurt she felt. She questioned Him, she railed at Him, and she cried healing tears at His feet.

HELPLESSNESS

Helplessness tells us we have no control. It's rooted in fear. It's a breeding ground for insecurity and feelings of inadequacy. Jesse never gained confidence in her ability to fend for herself in life, and she blamed her parents for not equipping her. Her dad loved her; he just didn't nurture her. Because he was all about following the rules and had a "my way or the highway" attitude, Jesse had no voice.

Her eating disorder wasn't about the food. It was about wanting someone to come to her rescue. Someone to hold and protect her. Someone to be the knight in shining armor. Jesse was still a small child looking for daddy to make things OK, but in so doing, she didn't grow up. Geneen Roth says this in her book *Women, Food and God:*

> As long as we take ourselves to be the child who was hurt by an unconscious parent, we will never grow up. We will never know who we actually are. We will keep looking for the parent who never

showed up and forget to see that the one who is
looking is no longer a child.[5]

If no one else is stepping up to the plate to protect us
in life, simply "being" is a scary place to live. We feel
alone. Isolated. Invisible. We feel we don't belong. No
wonder it's fertile ground for the Impostor to take over.

The truth is that while those helpless feelings of grief
and loss are painful, *they will not destroy us*. We are way
more resilient than we think.

Jesse believed she was helpless because she didn't think
she had what it took to live through the tough places of
life. To cope, she checked out through an eating disorder. Once she learned not to disconnect from herself
and to instead give herself a chance to grow, feel, and
express herself, she was able to see a different way to live.
It wasn't pain-free, but it was real.

Roth goes on to say that once we become aware of the
link we've created between "loneliness in the past and
aloneness in the present," we will be able to see that we're
"spending the present fearing what's already passed."[6]

Jesse finally realized she had to stop living in the past
bound to the "if onlys" of life. Once she identified the
losses of what she wanted but didn't get and was able to
put words to that pain, she was ready to risk moving on.

FEAR

Flashbacks. Night terrors. Body memories. Isolation.
Avoidance. All these things are the result of fear that's
been buried or left unattended. Looking through the lens

of abuse makes everything in the world seem unsafe. The trust needed to heal requires the victim do the very thing they cannot: open their hearts to another. When we can't do that, the loneliness of isolation washes over our souls, making the thin and worn places even more fragile.

The fear of whatever dreaded secret we're hiding being exposed causes us to withdraw. Wearing the masks assures us we won't be known. That's why we have to create the Impostor. Isolation and loss create fear, and most of us want to avoid what we're afraid of. But as we've seen, avoiding our fears is the worst thing we can do.

The following experiment is a good illustration of how a ubiquitous fear can take root in our hearts at a very young age and wreak havoc. This experiment was published in 1920 by psychologist Dr. John Watson and Rosalie Rayner, and it was conducted with the specific purpose of creating a fear or phobia in an emotionally stable child. Watson chose a nine-month-old child named Albert and exposed him to a series of stimuli: a white rat, a rabbit, a monkey, masks, and burning newspapers, and observed the boy's reactions. The boy initially showed no fear of any of the objects he was shown.

The next time Albert was exposed to the rat, Watson made a loud noise by hitting a metal pipe with a hammer. Naturally the child began to cry after hearing the loud noise. After repeatedly pairing the white rat with the loud noise, Albert began to cry simply after seeing the rat. Watson and Rayner wrote:

The instant the rat was shown, the baby began to cry. Almost instantly he turned sharply to the left, fell over on [his] left side, raised himself on all fours and began to crawl away so rapidly that he was caught with difficulty before reaching the edge of the table.[7]

What's the point? Seeing the rat, because he knew the noise would follow, traumatized little Albert. What often happens is that people become conditioned to be fearful of their own internal responses. They don't like the feelings, bodily responses, and sensations associated with the fear or phobia, so they avoid feeling or try to numb their pain. The thought or image of the traumatizing event can cause immobility. What is necessary is to separate the fear from the immobility. This restores control and helps to empower the individual.

Trauma isn't the only thing that creates terror. Remember I discovered Jesse's greatest fear early on in one of our sessions—the fear of being *alone*. That speaks to a loss of security. Alone is a big word. It tells us no one will be there. No one will take care of us. No one will protect us or stand by our side when the darkness comes. On a deeper level, it tells us that maybe we're not worth anyone being there.

Jesse didn't even recognize this fear until we dug deep into her belief system. She didn't want to admit it because then she would have to deal with the fact that she wasn't worth anyone wanting to care for her. Nonetheless, it was a catalyst that drove her eating-disordered behavior.

For her, it was about controlling something because she couldn't control the other thing happening.

As Jesse began to identify her losses and grieve them in healthy ways, the door to her heart began to open. Over time she would be open to the idea that what she believed about her self-worth was a lie. She also considered the possibility that even if no one was there for her, she was still totally secure in Christ. My job now was to pour the truth about God into her heart.

CONSIDER THIS

- What sorrows have you left unattended in your heart? What fears do you have about uncovering them?

- Is there unresolved anger or unattended sorrow you need to deal with? How has this affected your heart? How can you take some necessary first steps to deal with this?

- Have you felt forgotten by God? If so, how has that affected your relationship with Him?

- Do you fear being known? If so, why? Do you long to be known? If so, why?

- What losses did you identify with in this chapter? Have you grieved those losses? If not, are you willing to begin that process?

Chapter 7
THE TRUTH ABOUT GOD

I am God, and there is no one like Me.

—Isaiah **46:9**

OD IS UNIQUE. He isn't like anyone else we have ever had a relationship with, and that's part of our intrinsic problem. Because we expect people to let us down, betray us, or leave us, we automatically assume God will do the same. Therefore we are always on guard. We find it hard to trust. We expect others to want something from us. We go into relationships expecting them to fail, expecting to be hurt. So we humanize God, turn our feelings about Him into facts, and believe He will eventually abandon us as everyone else has.

If God is unique, we have to get used to the idea that the beliefs we've formed about relationship rules with others aren't going to apply to our relationship with God. Why? Because God doesn't think, respond, or react like anyone else we know. He has no needs. He doesn't manipulate. He relates unconditionally. He is full and complete. He's totally secure. He doesn't withdraw His love. He doesn't jump to conclusions. He knows everything about us, and He loves us still. He is a spirit being. When was the last time you had a friend like that?

The other people in our lives, even those closest to us,

were not meant to fill us. They can't. They won't. This is where we get it messed up. We look to others as our source and become disappointed when they don't measure up or meet our needs. That's how God wanted it. He didn't want other people to be life for us. He wants us to worship only Him.

Scripture says, "Those who worship Him must worship in spirit and truth" (John 4:24, NAS), but what does that mean anyway? It means those who worship God in spirit worship Him from the *heart*. They depend on Him for everything. For strength. For security. For adequacy. For unconditional love. For help in times of need. Their very sufficiency comes through Him. His life dwells within them, and through that life they draw from a never-ending source, a wellspring of life. They look to no other. He is the ever-present, self-existing God. Nothing takes Him by surprise. Nothing catches Him off guard. He is able to do immeasurably more than we can ask or imagine (Eph. 2:19–20).

We don't need ceremony, rules, or a particular place to worship God, as the Jews believed. Even though they worshipped the one true God (Ezra 4:2), they were idolaters:

> They worshiped the Lord, but they also served their own gods in accordance with customs of the nations from which they had been brought.
> —2 KINGS 17:33

Every relationship you have is a relationship with a needy person. Because of that, no one can relate without strings attached. We can't relate with *agape*. We can't relate without manipulating. Don't believe me? Take a look around you. Church. Marriage. Family. Friends. Work. Relationships get wounded and break up every day because of it.

Godly worship must be pure and sincere. It's the attitude of the heart that matters, not the place and not the ritual. Old Testament worship was clouded by ceremony and religious practices that were not pleasing to God:

> These people...honor me with their lips, but their
> hearts are far from me.
> —ISAIAH 29:13

In Matthew 15:9 Jesus condemns the corruption of the Jews' worship: "They worship me in vain; their teachings are but rules taught by men."

God isn't interested in rules; He's interested in a relationship, an intimate love relationship. Rules are about performance; relationship is about the heart. That's what I told Jesse. She was so tired of following all the rules that she loved what she was hearing. She had never thought about God in this way. She couldn't imagine Him loving her in spite of her mess-ups or in spite of all her shortcomings.

How about you—are you tired of religion? Feeling spiritually bankrupt? Tired of trying to follow all the rules and do everything right, thinking God still isn't happy with your performance? Then consider this: Maybe it's time to start breaking the rules. Heretical thought? Not really. Jesse grew up in a family that was more interested in the rules of religion than in a personal relationship with a living being. The result was she never knew or felt known by God. If you've ever felt the same way, than maybe you've had a relationship with religion and not with Jesus. What's the answer? Realizing that Jesus's performance on the cross was the only performance necessary to reconcile us to God. Our job is to give Him full access to our hearts and see what happens.

How Is God Different?

It's important to understand how God is different from anything else we've ever known because if we're going to have a relationship with Him, we have to understand His heart. That will determine how we respond to Him. How do we experience the heart of God? By reading the stories in the Bible that reveal who He is. Loving. Compassionate. Forgiving. Healer. Savior. Comforter. Creator. We do it by communing with Him moment by moment. By spending time with Him. By allowing ourselves to intentionally practice His presence.

When we do that, we discover some of these things about God.

God is full and complete.

God needs nothing apart from Himself to be secure. This is important because God needs nothing from us. Because He has no needs, He can relate to us with unconditional, unfailing love and without an expectation of getting anything back from us. God doesn't have some ulterior motive to love us, and He isn't waiting to withdraw His love from us for not being perfect and keeping all the rules.

At first, this concept of God was hard for Jesse to grasp. She couldn't imagine a relationship where someone didn't expect something back from her. Because she didn't trust easily, this made relationships more difficult for her. I explained to her that God uses a grace-based operating system with us. That means we get what we don't deserve for free!

God is unchanging.

God always remains the constant in our lives. When our feelings change, when our circumstances change, or when life throws us off balance, God is still the same. He doesn't get tired of listening to us. He doesn't need a temporary separation. Our constant whining and complaining don't annoy Him. And He doesn't change like the shifting shadows. That is important if you have abandonment or insecurity issues as Jesse did, because God doesn't leave us for a better offer. He's in the trenches with us for the long haul.

God is full.

Because God lives in us, we are full. The trouble is, we don't feel like we're full, so we assume we're operating from a sense of loss or deficit. Scripture reminds us, "For in Christ all the fullness of the Deity lives in bodily form, and in Christ you have been brought to fullness" (Col. 2:9–10).

Fullness is a prerequisite for unconditional love. That's

why unconditional love is dependent on the fullness of the one giving it, not the performance of the one receiving it.

If we are God's children, we are full because His life fills us moment by moment. If, however, I don't believe I'm full, if I think I'm lacking something, just as Eve did in the garden or Jenny Lauren did on the runway, then I will try to get someone or something else to fill me. That something else is what causes us to use the masks we wear to get what we need. You see, you and I were never created to live out of our own resources (our flesh). We were created to live out of the life of another (Christ). When we live from Christ, when we depend on Him moment by moment, not only will He meet all our needs, but He will also fill us to overflowing!

God is all-sufficient.

The "I Am" is the all-sufficient one. He always was and always will be. *Ego eimi* is the first-person singular present tense of the Greek verb *to be* or *to exist*. This is God's way of telling us through His name that He is our strong tower, our mighty defense, and the Lion of Judah. If He is all-sufficient, we have nothing to fear.

God is eternal.

God is the only being that has no beginning and no end. He is eternal. When we think of eternal life, we think of life in heaven with Jesus or something we get when we become Christian. And while that's true, eternal life affords us even more than a life in heaven after we die. Eternal life is the person of the Lord Jesus Christ, and when we become believers, we enter into that eternal life. We enter into Christ's life. It's something we partake of. It's something that affords us everything we need for life.

Because you and I were born into life in Adam, God had to make provision for us to die to one identity and be born into another. He did that through Christ's death on the cross:

> That which was from the beginning, which we have heard, which we have seen with our eyes, which we have looked at and our hands have touched—this we proclaim concerning the Word of life. The life appeared; we have seen it and testify to it, and we proclaim to you the eternal life, which was with the Father and has appeared to us.
>
> —1 JOHN 1:1–2

> We know also that the Son of God has come and has given us understanding, so that we may know him who is true. And we are in him who is true by being in his Son Jesus Christ. He is the true God and eternal life.
>
> —1 JOHN 5:20

How exciting to know that we partake of an already existing eternal life!

God is a giver by nature.

If God is a giver by nature, it stands to reason that He made us to be receivers of His life. That means He is a Father who wants to give us good gifts:

117

> Every good and perfect gift is from above, coming down from the Father of the heavenly lights, who does not change like shifting shadows.
>
> —JAMES 1:17

Giving is consistent with God's nature and character:

> So I say to you: Ask and it will be given to you; seek and you will find; knock and the door will be opened to you. For everyone who asks receives; the one who seeks finds; and to the one who knocks, the door will be opened. Which of you fathers, if your son asks for a fish, will give him a snake instead? Or if he asks for an egg, will give him a scorpion? If you then, though you are evil, know how to give good gifts to your children, how much more will your Father in heaven give the Holy Spirit to those who ask him!
>
> —LUKE 11:9–13

God has a different operating system.

God relates to us out of a grace-based operating system. *Grace* means "unmerited favor," and because this is how God relates, His focus is on our *being*, not our *doing*. That's hard for us to grasp. When we come to God, we come with an attitude of "God, what can I do to get You to like me a little better?" When we first become Christians, we accept the free gift of salvation, but as time goes on, we find ourselves working, striving, and trying hard to get God's approval, when His desire is that we come as we are. We already have His approval, and it's not based on anything we've done or not done!

This doesn't mean God doesn't care about our behavior.

He does. He wants us to follow His precepts. But He is perfectly willing for us to blow it. His love is unchanging when we blow it, and He will allow us to experience the consequences of our sin. As a loving parent, He waits patiently for us to repent and turn back to Him.

How We're Cut Off

When Adam and Eve sinned in the garden, they were cut off from the source of life. They entered into a death system (Gen. 2:16–17). This means they died spiritually.

What does spiritual death mean, and how does it impact us? It means the absence of God's life—all the things we were promised in 2 Peter 1:3:

> His divine power has given us everything we need for a godly life through our knowledge of him who called us by his own glory and goodness.

It looks something like this:

Life System	Death System
Security	Worthlessness
Love	Insecurity
Peace	Inadequacy
Acceptance	Hate
Freedom	Unforgiveness
Value/worth	Anxiety
Adequacy	Emptiness
Forgiveness	Rejection
Fullness	Try harder
Rest	Bondage

Without the true source of life, Adam and Eve had to come up with some other way to get a sense of life. In other words, they had to build a false life source. Enter a workable Impostor called the *flesh*. The Greek word for *flesh* in Scripture is *sarx*. For our purposes, *flesh* is defined like this:

> (*sarks*) is generally negative, referring to making decisions (actions) *according to self* – i.e. done *apart from faith* (independent from God's working). Thus what is "*of the flesh (carnal)*" is by definition displeasing to the Lord – even things that *seem* "respectable!" In short, *flesh* generally relates to *unaided human effort,* i.e. decisions (actions) that originate from self or are empowered by self. This is *carnal* ("of the *flesh*") and proceeds out of the *untouched (unchanged)* part of us – i.e. what is *not* transformed by God.[1]

First Corinthians 1:26 says:

> Brothers and sisters, think of what you were when you were called. Not many of you were wise by human standards; not many were influential; not many were of noble birth.

If we look at Paul's discourse in Philippians 3:3–8, we see the flesh can appear respectable:

> For it is we who are the circumcision, we who serve God by his Spirit, who boast in Christ Jesus, and who put no confidence in the flesh— though I myself have reasons for such confidence. If

someone else thinks they have reasons to put confidence in the flesh, I have more: circumcised on the eighth day, of the people of Israel, of the tribe of Benjamin, a Hebrew of Hebrews; in regard to the law, a Pharisee; as for zeal, persecuting the church; as for righteousness based on the law, faultless. But whatever were gains to me I now consider loss for the sake of Christ. What is more, I consider everything a loss because of the surpassing worth of knowing Christ Jesus my Lord, for whose sake I have lost all things.

Paul had it all going on. He was smart, educated, talented, and successful—and all the things he looked to in order to make life work ended up becoming rubbish to him for the sake of knowing Christ. In fact, it was those very things that separated him from Christ. That's what the flesh does—it keeps us from depending on Christ. Does this sound familiar? By now you should be making the connection between the flesh and the Impostor. The flesh is a false hope. It's a counterfeit. It can't provide real life for us.

In Jeremiah 2:13 God uses the analogy of a cistern (a hole in the ground to catch water) to rebuke the children of Israel for looking to their flesh as a source of life instead of looking to the spring of living water: "My people have committed two sins: They have forsaken me, the spring of living water, and have dug their own cisterns, broken cisterns that cannot hold water."

When we dig cisterns, we can never rest. We have to keep digging, keep trying harder, and keep performing.

Jesse lived her entire life looking to other things as her source instead of looking to them as resources. She was tired of digging cisterns. She was ready to hear the truth about God.

THE NATURE OF GOD

God reveals His character through the written Word and through the person of the Lord Jesus Christ. The first thing Jesse and I talked about was the goodness of God. It's hard to bring congruence to a good God and a traumatic event in our lives. We have to take Scripture at its word, and so Jesse and I looked at the following verses:

> Give thanks to the LORD, for he is good; his love endures forever.
> —1 CHRONICLES 16:34

> For the LORD is good and his love endures forever; his faithfulness continues through all generations.
> —PSALM 100:5

> Taste and see that the LORD is good; blessed is the one who takes refuge in him.
> —PSALM 34:8

> The lions may grow weak and hungry but those who seek the LORD lack no good thing.
> —PSALM 34:10

> Behold, I have inscribed you on the palms of My hands; Your walls are continually before Me.
> —ISAIAH 49:16, NKJV

The LORD's lovingkindnesses indeed never cease.... They are new every morning; great is Your faithfulness.

—LAMENTATIONS 3:22–23, NAS

Deciding about the goodness of God requires us to think about the definition of the word *good*. God's definition of good is different from ours. For us, good means my life is relatively problem free, things turn out the way I want them to, and the story has a happy ending. The problem is that we are on Planet Earth, and nobody gets out of here alive.

Jesse was confronted with deciding if God could still be good even though she suffered loss. If she continued to believe lies about God's character, she would have no other recourse but to depend on her flesh.

It's risky to surrender because it requires that we trust God with total abandon. Fear begins to wash over us at the mere thought of it, paralyzing and immobilizing us. It is here, however, in the crucible of suffering that what we believe about the heart of God determines the path we will take. Convinced of God's goodness, we will press into the heart of the Savior through the grit and grime of heartbreak and loss. Unconvinced, we buy into a host of lies that God is unloving, unmerciful, or just doesn't care.

Kay Arthur, in her devotional study *Lord, I Want to Know You*, talks about the powerful name of God as El Elyon. Kay says, "If God is not sovereign, if He is not in control, if all things are not under His dominion, then He is not the Most High, and you and I are either in the hands of fate (whatever that is), in the hands of man, or in the hands of the devil."[2]

THE NAMES OF GOD

We can learn a lot about a person, a place, or a thing simply by its name. For example, think about a place called Horsethief Canyon. Or how about Bloody Basin? If you close your eyes, you can conjure up some pretty wild images to match those names. That's the cool thing about a name—it tells a story about something.

God's name does the same thing for us—only He gets to have lots of different names to tell us the story of His heart. He did it that way so we won't have to guess what He's like. He did it that way so we could be sure of Him, so we would know He is good and that His heart toward us is good, even when bad things happen. That's why He sent His only Son—so that we would know He doesn't require anything from us He wasn't willing to walk through Himself—again and again and again. God reveals Himself as three persons with one spirit life—God the Father, Jesus the Son, and the Holy Spirit.

Elohim

Elohim is the name that tells us God is our Creator. *El* in Scripture means "mighty, power, or prominent" and is always used as a reference for God. *Him* is signifi-cant because it suggests plurality—Father, Son, and Holy Spirit: three persons; one spirit life. In the Pentateuch the name *Elohim* suggests God is a transcendent being and the Creator of the universe.[3] What incredible news! The three mighty persons of the Trinity are doing battle on our behalf. God created us intentionally; our birth wasn't an accident, even if we feel we don't belong, even if we feel we don't matter, even if we feel we're unlovable. God, the mighty Creator of the entire universe, adores us.

Jehovah

Jehovah is translated as "the existing One" or "Lord." The chief meaning of *Jehovah* is derived from the Hebrew word *Havah*, meaning "to be" or "to exist." It also suggests "to become" or specifically "to become known." This denotes a God who reveals Himself unceasingly.[4]

El Roi

Do you ever feel invisible? Hagar sure did. She was the maidservant of Sarah in the Old Testament Book of Genesis. Here's her story: She was given to Abraham to conceive the child that Sarah, his wife, could not bear. When Hagar became pregnant, she began to despise her mistress, Sarah. She felt dismissed, unlovable, used, and invisible. Sarah, sensing Hagar's attitude, consulted with Abraham, and he advised her to do with Hagar as she wished. Sarah dealt harshly with Hagar, causing Hagar to flee from her homeland.

Hagar fled into the desert. On her way an angel of the Lord appeared to her. He instructed her to return to Sarah so that she may bear Abraham a child. She was told to call her son Ishmael. Hagar referred to God as *El Roi*, meaning "the God who sees," because He had heard her cry and answered (Gen. 16:13).

We can have confidence that no matter what we are facing, God sees us and is sensitive to our plight. We are not invisible to *El Roi*. We are not in danger of harm. The Creator of the universe sees us and watches over us every moment. Listen to Psalm 121:1–4:

> I lift up my eyes to the mountains—where does my help come from? My help comes from the LORD, the Maker of heaven and earth. He will not let your foot slip—he who watches over you will not slumber; indeed, he who watches over Israel will neither slumber nor sleep.

Jesse was finally able to look through a different lens as she considered the character of God and weighed it against her abuse. She had spent so many years trying to figure it all out when the truth is, none of us will have all the answers to the difficult things of life—not to mention that answers don't provide the freedom we believe they will. The real question to consider is: Can we move forward and live in spite of the not knowing?

My friend Cecil Murphey says this in his book *Making Sense When Life Doesn't*:

> I don't understand pain; I don't understand suffering, but I'm alive and my life has meaning.[5]

That's what Jesse was beginning to see: Her life *did* have meaning. There was a greater purpose beyond what she had ever considered. Something God had created her for. A story that only she could tell. Later we will explore how she was going to be able to use that story for a redemptive purpose.

Jehovah Shammah

> Piglet sidled up to Pooh from behind. "Pooh," he whispered.
> "Yes, Piglet?"
> "Nothing," said Piglet, taking Pooh's paw. "I just wanted to be sure of you."[6]

That scene between Pooh and Piglet is an attachment moment—one human being reaching for another and asking, "Will you be there for me? Do I matter to you? Will you respond to me if I need you?" If the answer is no, according to our old friend John Bowlby, we are wired to respond with fear, anxiety, or anger. That anxiety we feel becomes heightened if we believe we are alone. It's a core fear.

Think about it. If you're trapped in a dark place, there is no foreseeable way out, you're all alone, and someone or something is coming after you, what are your chances of making it out alive? Not good. What's the point? From a survival perspective, the point is how well you try to fight to try and make it out alive.

But think back to attachment theory for a minute. Attachment theory would add to the idea of doing battle this piece: If you have someone standing beside you, something changes. The battle doesn't look so hopeless. The darkness isn't so black. The demons aren't so big. Who's with you makes all the difference in the world.

Jesus is with you. He is *Jehovah Shammah*—the Lord is there.

In Ezekiel 48:35 *Jehovah Shammah* is used as a reference to the earthly Jerusalem. The name indicates that God has not abandoned His chosen one. He will not leave her in ruins but will restore her once again. Boy, did that get Jesse's attention. Feeling like her life had been in ruins for so long, she actually began to believe restoration was possible, even for her.

The word *shammah* means "there." We can count on God being there for us at all times because He gave us His Spirit to dwell inside us. We don't have to wait for heaven. We have the assurance from this name of God that He is there for us right now, whenever we call on Him.

Adonai Mekoddishkem

In the Old Testament, *Jehovah Mekoddishkem* occurs two times and is partly derived from the Hebrew word *qâdash*, meaning "sanctify," "holy," or "set apart." *Jehovah Mekoddishkem* can be translated as "the Lord who sets you apart."[7]

Jesse saw that being set apart meant she was special. She had always looked to the eating disorder as a way to see herself as unique. Now she was beginning to see that God Himself had created her, set her apart, and was there even through her most harrowing ordeal. She was beginning to understand that He purposefully used His names in Scripture as a way to assure us of His nature and character so that when the darkness starts to close in, we will know. We will trust. We will not lose heart.

Jehovah Jireh

Jehovah Jireh is a symbolic name given on Mount Moriah by Abraham to memorialize God's provision of a substitute for the sacrifice of his son Isaac in Genesis 22:14. The name *Jehovah Jireh* in the Old Testament literally means "the Lord will see" or "the Lord will provide," meaning He will give a means of deliverance.[8] It means that because God is omniscient and omnipresent, He sees and foresees all our needs and provides for them accordingly.

We can sing about Jehovah Jireh all we want in church, but where the rubber meets the road, does that feeling translate into a belief that God can and will meet all our needs? That's where we struggle. Abraham was so convinced of the goodness of God that he was raising the knife to kill his son. That's faith. That's trust. That's belief in the goodness of God.

Jehovah Shalom

It's not unlike God to use the least likely person to accomplish the greatest tasks. We see this with David, a shepherd boy, through his killing of the mighty Goliath, and we come across it again in the Old Testament account of Gideon. This is where we encounter God as *Jehovah Shalom*. This name occurs only once, in Judges 6:22–24 (KJV), where an angel appears to the young

Gideon, instructing him to deliver Israel from the hand of the Midianites.

Gideon said, "'O Lord, how shall I deliver Israel? Behold, my family is the least in Manasseh, and I am the youngest in my father's house.' But the LORD said to him, 'Surely I will be with you, and you shall defeat Midian as one man'" (Judg. 6:15-16, NAS). Gideon was afraid when he realized this was an angel of the Lord. He said:

> "Alas, O Lord GOD! For now I have seen the angel of the LORD face to face." The LORD said to him, "Peace to you, do not fear; you shall not die." Then Gideon built an altar there to the LORD and named it The LORD is Peace.
> —JUDGES 6:22–24, NAS

Peace—real peace—can only be found in Christ. We all say we believe that, but when we're being buffeted by the storms of life, most of us don't experience it. We have to be convinced of two things: first, that no matter what happens, God is in control; and second, that His heart toward us is good. Take a look:

> "For I know the plans I have for you," declares the LORD, "plans to prosper you and not to harm you, to give you a future and a hope."
> —JEREMIAH 29:11

Jehovah Rapha

Rapha means "to restore," "to heal," or "to make healthful" in Hebrew. This name for God can be translated as "Jehovah who heals." Here, Jehovah is the Great

Physician who heals the physical and emotional needs of His people.[9]

When Jesse heard this, she took a deep breath.

"If that's true, why hasn't God healed me?" she moaned. "He could take all this away in a second if He wanted to," she moaned.

"God is more interested in conforming us to His image than in making us happy," I told her. "He sees your pain. He saw your abuse. And here's what we know about that: God will judge and punish those who hurt you."

Take a look:

> Jesus said to his disciples: "Things that cause people to stumble are bound to come, but woe to anyone through whom they come. It would be better for them to be thrown into the sea with a millstone tied around their neck than to cause one of these little ones to stumble."
>
> —Luke 17:1–2

I told Jesse that God's desire before she was even born was to fill her heart to overflowing. To drive the point home, I did a little demonstration for her. I took a clear glass and a pitcher of water and placed them side by side. Slowly I poured the water into the glass, asking Jesse what she noticed.

"The glass is filling up with water," she said.

"What would happen if I kept pouring all the water from this pitcher into the glass?" I asked.

"It would overflow," she said.

"Right, and overflowing is the fullness you possess in

Christ. Now, as you watched the water being poured into this glass, is there any place on the glass that it hasn't touched?"

"No."

"So you're telling me that the glass has been immersed by every molecule of water?"

"Yes. Absolutely."

"You see, Jesse," I said, speaking quietly, "it's only the places we surrender that God can fill. If I dammed up the glass, the water couldn't flow to all the empty places in it. God wants to fill your heart moment by moment to overflowing, but He can't do that if you insist on walling some of the empty places off. He won't demand control. You can't have it both ways."

"So what you're telling me is that fullness is my birthright?" she asked.

"Absolutely!"

CONSIDER THIS

- What lies have you believed about God, past or present?

- What feelings have you had about God over time?

- What is your favorite name for God? Why?

- What does it mean to you that God remains unchanging in your life?

- If God is full and complete and we are in Him, can you see yourself as full too? If not, why?

- Do you believe the Lord is near? What difference would it make in your life if you did?

- What places have you walled off in your heart in the name of control? How willing are you now to allow the Lord to fill those places?

- Have you looked at your relationship with God as being primarily about following the rules or about an intimate relationship?

Chapter 8
WHO'S YOUR DADDY?

*Because you are sons, God sent the Spirit of his Son
into our hearts, the Spirit who calls out, "Abba, Father."
So you are no longer a slave, but a son; and since
you are a son, God has made you also an heir.*
—**GALATIANS 4:6–7**

I N THE OPENING chapters of this book I suggested the
reason people hide their true selves—the reason they
wear masks and create an Impostor to cope with life,
solve their problems, and get their needs met—is because
they don't know who they really are. We looked at the
game show *To Tell the Truth*, and we saw that the real
problem with the two impostors on the show who tried
to fool the audience and judges into believing they were
the authentic central character was that they didn't have
a birth certificate to prove they *were* the central character.

What does a birth certificate prove? This is a silly
question, I know. A birth certificate proves who you are.
It authenticates your name. My name before I was married was Rita Alesandrelli. It's Italian. I didn't choose
it. I didn't go through a list of Italian names and pick
it out. I had nothing to do with it. More importantly,
there is absolutely nothing I can do to change the fact
that I'm an Alesandrelli. Even though I'm married and

my surname has changed, all my genetics confirm I'm still an Alesandrelli.

I am an Alesandrelli because my father was an Alesandrelli and my grandfather before him. Whether I act like an Alesandrelli or not, I am still an Alesandrelli. If I go to Timbuktu, I'm an Alesandrelli. If I stay in Virginia, I'm an Alesandrelli. Even though I married Michael Schulte, I don't have Schulte genetics. I don't have Schulte identity. In other words, no matter how hard I might try to behave like my husband, my identity doesn't change. Why? Because my identity has nothing to do with my behavior or how I act. The only thing that counts is the birth certificate. Identity is determined by birth, and my birthright determines what I am entitled to.

God tells us that as believers we possess a unique birthright—one that gives us value, perfection, security, adequacy, acceptance, and a limitless supply of unconditional love. This inheritance we have can never perish, spoil, or fade. It's kept in heaven for us, but we can experience the victory this identity affords us here on earth by understanding some things about our birthright.

This birthright invites us to be the bride of Christ. It invites us to believe the unbelievable about who we are: no longer dirty, rotten sinners but saints beloved by God. We are made in His image. We are His workmanship. That didn't change even when everything went south in the garden to cause all this mess.

NOTHING BUT PROBLEMS

We get that we have a problem. We inherited it from Adam. Actually, we inherited *three* problems. Let's take them one by one.

The first problem is sin. Isaiah 59:2 says, "Your iniquities [sins] have separated you from your God." No big news flash there. The second problem, however, seems a bit more radical: We have a dead spirit. This means we don't have spirit life from God. And the third problem is the flesh—our coping strategies.

Our birth into Adam made us sinners. It wasn't because we were the ones who originally sinned; it was because the whole human race was *in* Adam when *he* sinned. We didn't choose it. We can't change it. If we trace our gene pool all the way back to our great-great-great-grandfathers and all the way back to Adam, we will see that we were "in Adam's loins" when he sinned in the garden. That means everything that happened to Adam spiritually happened to us, according to Romans 5:12.

Here is what we notice about the identity we inherited in Adam:

- When Adam sinned, we sinned: "Therefore, just as sin entered the world through one man, and death through sin, and in this way death came to all people, because all sinned" (Rom. 5:12).

- When Adam died spiritually, we died spiritually: "...many died by the trespass of the one man" (v. 15).

- When Adam was condemned, we were condemned: "Consequently, just as one trespass resulted in condemnation for all people, so also one righteous act resulted in justification and life for all people" (v. 18).

- When Adam became a sinner, we became sinners. "For just as through the disobedience of the one man the many were made sinners, so also through the obedience of the one man the many will be made righteous" (v. 19).

- God took care of our sin problem with Christ's death on the cross: "In whom we have redemption through His blood, even the forgiveness of sins" (Col. 1:14, NKJV). Furthermore, "But if we walk in the light as He is in the light, we have fellowship with one another, and the blood of Jesus Christ His Son cleanses us from all sin" (1 John 1:7, NKJV).

Sin problem—done.

Next up, we have a dead, unregenerate spirit. What does that mean? When Adam and Eve sinned, they lost spirit life from God. What did He tell them in the garden? The Lord God commanded the man, saying:

> From any tree of the garden you may eat freely; but
> from the tree of the knowledge of good and evil
> you shall not eat, for in the day that you eat form
> it *you will surely die.*
> —GENESIS 2:16–17, NAS, EMPHASIS ADDED

Adam and Eve chose to rebel. They chose independence instead of dependence. They lost spirit life. They were dead.

> And you were dead in your trespasses and sins, in
> which you formerly walked according to the course
> of this world, according to the prince of the power
> of the air, of the spirit that is now working in the
> sons of disobedience. Among them we too all for-
> merly lived in the lusts of our flesh, indulging the
> desires of the flesh and of the mind, and were by
> *nature children of wrath, even as the rest.*
> —EPHESIANS 2:1–3, NAS, EMPHASIS ADDED

This word *nature* determines our identity. We were born into life in Adam as children of wrath. Unregenerate. Sinners. Cut off from the true source of life. Our first parents had to find some other way to find a pseudo source of life, a false life—the Impostor—so they looked within themselves to their own resources and found their masks. The problem was they only had their flesh left to depend on. This "nature" led them to the coping strategies—masks—we all develop apart from Christ:

> For the flesh desires what is contrary to the Spirit,
> and the Spirit what is contrary to the flesh. They

are in conflict with each other so that you do not
do whatever you want.

—Galatians 5:17

What does a dead person need? Life. How does he get
it? An exchange has to be made. While we didn't choose
to be born into life in Adam and there was nothing we
could do to change it, God had a plan of escape for us, the
only one that would work. The sacrifice had to be perfect.
The victim had to be sinless. The debt had to be paid in
full. God made a promise. He sent His Son. He paid the
price for freedom. He made the greatest exchange in the
history of mankind.

> For God so loved the world he gave his one and
> only son.
>
> —John 3:16

> But because of his great love for us, God, who is
> rich in mercy, made us alive with Christ even when
> we were dead in transgressions—it is by grace you
> have been saved.
>
> —Ephesians 2:4–5

> If Christ is in you, though the body is dead
> because of sin, yet the spirit is alive because of
> righteousness.
>
> —Romans 8:10, nas

The only way you and I can get rid of our old identity in Adam and get a new birthright is by death—not
physical death, but spiritual death. Remember that the

death Adam was to die, according to God's Word, was a spiritual death.

MOVING ON UP

We have to get out of Adam and get into Christ. How does that happen? Through the free gift of salvation. God did it through Christ. All we have to do is receive it and enter into His life. The same way we were born into Adam's seed because we were *in him* when he sinned, we were *in Christ* when He died on the cross. Watchman Nee explains this idea in his book *The Normal Christian Life:* "When the Lord Jesus was on the cross all of us died—not individually because we had not yet been born—but being in him we died in him. 'One died for all, therefore, all died' (2 Cor. 5:14)."[1]

Nee goes on to illustrate this principle by sharing how he explained it to the Chinese people in the village:

> I remember once I took a small book and put a piece of paper into it, and I said to those very simple folk, "Now look carefully. I take a piece of paper. It has an identity of its own, quite separate from this book. Having no special purpose for it at the moment I put it into the book. Now I do something with the book. I mail it to Shanghai. I do not mail the paper, but the paper has been put into the book. Then where is the paper? Can the book go to Shanghai and the paper remain here? Can the paper have a separate destiny from the book? No! Where the book goes the paper goes. If I drop the book in the river the paper goes too, and if I

quickly take it out again I recover the paper also. Whatever experience the book goes through the paper goes through with it, for it is still there in the book."[2]

First Corinthians 1:30 says this: "It is because of him [God] that you are in Christ Jesus." Galatians 2:20 also makes this clear: "I have been crucified with Christ and I no longer live, but Christ lives in me. The life I now live in the body, I live by faith in the Son of God, who loved me and gave himself for me."

To be identified with Christ, we had to go through what He went through. Not only did we die with Him (because we are in His seed when we become believers), but we were also buried and resurrected with Him, as stated in Romans 6:4–5:

> We were therefore buried with him through baptism into death in order that, just as Christ was raised from the dead through the glory of the Father, we too may live a new life. For if we have been united with him in a death like his, we will certainly also be united with him in a resurrection like his.

Talk about amazing! When Christ was crucified, we were crucified. It was *past tense*. It is finished. *Tetelasti*—the last word Jesus uttered from the cross as He gave up His spirit and died. It is finished. The great exchange was made. The debt was satisfied. We were made new. The sin barrier was removed. God resurrects our dead spirit and gives us His life. That means we are alive to Christ and dead to the power of sin as our master.

Paul says in Ephesians 2:4–5:

> But because of his great love for us, God, who is rich in mercy, made us alive with Christ even when we were dead in transgressions—it is by grace you have been saved.

He also says in Romans 5:10:

> For if, while we were God's enemies, we were reconciled to him through the death of his Son, how much more, having been reconciled, shall we be saved through his life!

The other amazing thing we've been given through this new birth is the mind of Christ (1 Cor. 2:16). That means we have the power to refute the lies of the enemy and take every thought captive to the obedience of Christ. We don't have to try hard to do it, for His life in us does it. All we have to do is pay attention to what we're believing and be intentional about renewing our minds (more on that to come).

The only remaining problem you and I still have to contend with is the flesh. While we have been freed from the power of sin, we are still prone to wander. We are still prone to erecting idols. We can chose to commit sin, though, as Galatians 5:16 warns us:

> So I say, walk by the Spirit, and you will not gratify the desires of the flesh.

Also:

> Do not use your freedom to indulge in the flesh.
> —GALATIANS 5:13

At this point in my work with Jesse it was pretty evident to her that she had become a master at walking after the flesh. The interesting thing about the flesh, though, is that it doesn't have to look *bad*. Take a look at Paul as he talks about his good-looking flesh:

> For it is we who are the circumcision, we who serve God by his Spirit, who boast in Christ Jesus, and who put no confidence in the flesh—though I myself have reasons for such confidence. *If someone else thinks they have reasons to put confidence in the flesh, I have more: circumcised on the eighth day, of the people of Israel, of the tribe of Benjamin, a Hebrew of Hebrews; in regard to the law, a Pharisee; as for zeal, persecuting the church; as for righteousness based on the law, faultless.* But whatever were gains to me I now consider loss for the sake of Christ. What is more, I consider everything a loss because of the surpassing worth of knowing Christ Jesus my Lord, for whose sake I have lost all things. I consider them garbage, that I may gain Christ.
> —PHILIPPIANS 3:3–8, EMPHASIS ADDED

Paul, like many of us, had some great things going for him. He could have been *Time* magazine's man of the year, having come from the best family, gotten the best education, and been one of the few that could keep the law perfectly. The problem is that when we have good-looking flesh, it's hard for us to see our neediness. It's hard for us to see how we're depending on our masks instead of Christ.

How did God finally get Paul's attention? He had to blind him on the Damascus road. He had to give Paul a new heart. The flesh doesn't need to be cleaned up, beloved. It needs to be crucified! Changing one bad flesh pattern or coping strategy to one that's a little more acceptable—like swapping anger for self-righteousness—isn't the answer. The answer is to deal a deathblow to the flesh altogether.

How do we do that? By being convinced it doesn't work anymore. By seeing and admitting that it doesn't provide what we really need. That it's only a temporary fix. That it keeps us focused on self. That it causes us to wear masks. That it causes us to create an Impostor. We have to ask ourselves: Do we really want to keep living like this?

Jesse didn't. She was tired of not being loved for who she really was. She was tired of pretending she had life all figured out and was problem free. She was tired of trying to keep all the balls in the air. She was tired of running. She needed someone else to depend on. Someone she could really trust. Someone who would never leave. She needed a new way. She needed what she was entitled to because of her *real* birthright.

FULLY ALIVE

I asked Jesse in one of our sessions, "Have you ever felt fully alive?" Then I read her this quote from David Needham's book *Birthright*:

> What is it that determines how fully alive any person is? What needs to happen during the span of our lives so that at the end of it all we can look back and say, "I have truly lived!" I believe there are two things people require... *We must fulfill the destiny for which we were made* while at the same time *being true to who we are*.[3]

Jesse was sad she had lived for so many years not being authentic. She was beginning to realize she had never really lived the life she was called to live. As the wise King Solomon declared, "So I hated life, because what is done under the sun was grievous to me; all of it is meaningless, a chasing after the wind" (Eccles. 2:17). Solomon had everything life could offer: riches, possessions, land, pleasure, beauty, and fame. But in the end, he found them all meaningless. They didn't satisfy. He still came up empty. He still missed being fully alive.

Think about that for a minute. We're talking about a king. He had everything—literally everything—this world could offer. But he still wasn't happy.

Now think about your own life. What is it you want or believe you need in order to be happy? Have you ever gotten something you really wanted, something you waited to get for a long time, only to have its luster fade in a few months?

You don't have to have an eating disorder as Jesse did to have a feeling of deep emptiness invading your soul. If you've spent a lifetime struggling to be perfect, trying hard to gain the acceptance of others, or believing you aren't measuring up, you're probably really tired. And maybe, just maybe, you're considering that what *you* thought was life isn't really life at all.

If that's the case, you're ready to consider a new way. You're ready to give up on the flesh to discover the real meaning and purpose in your life. That journey will require some rebuilding. It requires ridding ourselves of the secrets and the shame that have so easily entangled us. So put on your hard hat, and let's begin the journey.

CONSIDER THIS

- What flesh patterns do you struggle with— pleasing, trying harder, control?

- What has been the payoff for you in these flesh patterns?

- Have you given up on the workings of your flesh?

- What does it mean to have your identity in Christ?

- What happened to you at the cross?

- How could understanding your true birthright impact your life?

- Have you lived an authentic life? If not, what needs to happen to change that?

- King Solomon had everything money could buy, and he said it was all vanity, a chasing after the wind. What things have you chased after that you believed would make you happy, only to find you came up empty?

Chapter 9
THE HEART OF THE PROBLEM

*Those who look to him are radiant; their
faces are never covered with shame.*
—PSALM 34:5

JESSE CAME FROM a successful family, and on the surface everything seemed picture perfect. Her parents loved their kids, but they placed very high expectations on them, especially Jesse. Without realizing it, they communicated the message that in order to be somebody, you had to do something extraordinary. You could not settle for being mediocre. Jesse interpreted that to mean she had to become someone of notoriety. As we've seen, the pressure of trying to live up to unrealistic standards can be a train wreck waiting to happen.

Jesse's father was a hard driver. He was the Type A personality on steroids, and he would often lose his temper. He didn't have the first clue how to repair the ruptures in his relationships, so he didn't. This left Jesse filled with shame. To avoid those feelings, she would disconnect through not eating. Because no one ever stepped in to show her how to regulate the feelings of hurt, rejection, and the shame she felt, she learned to depend on the only thing she knew: her flesh.

The truth was, Jesse couldn't overcome the nagging

feeling deep within her heart that told her something was inherently wrong with her. It was the voice of shame. Shame not only tells us we're inadequate because of what we've done or failed to do, but it also tells us we're intrinsically bad and unlovable. It's an embodied experience, meaning we not only perceive it as a fact but we feel and experience it in every fiber of our being. To avoid shame's paralyzing sensations, we'll do just about anything—including deny we have a problem at all.

That's why it's far easier to create an Impostor.

But how did a girl like Jesse—young, beautiful, smart, someone who appeared to have it all together—end up being filled with shame? Was she too introspective, or was there something more percolating below the conscious surface?

Children are the best recorders of information but the worst interpreters of it. Their brains record and encode both verbal and nonverbal cues from significant people in their lives. This means that long before they are able to put words to what's happening in their hearts—long before they can even logically process an event or think abstractly—they can experience the feelings of shame through a harsh tone, a disgusting glance, or a roll of the eyes. Over time, if those experiences are repeated, a child not knowing how to cope with these shaming experiences will develop a set of coping strategies—masks— that will enable him or her to disengage from the felt experience of being shamed.

Jesse tried hard to do just that. She recounted one of

the first experiences she remembered of feeling shamed by her father to me in one of our sessions.

"My dad publicly embarrassed me because I failed to score a goal in my soccer tournament," she said. "I'll never forget it. He grabbed my arm and rebuked me harshly in front of my teammates for not doing my best: 'You've got to try harder, Jesse. Don't you get that? You're always blowing it when it counts. You'll never amount to anything if you don't perform. You don't want to be a loser, do you?' I was six years old."

Jesse was humiliated in front of her friends, so she made a vow. Vows are simply the heart's attempt to control pain. They can be conscious or unconscious, but their job is simple: to help us divert, deny, or diffuse the thoughts that threaten to shame or undo us. We promise ourselves we will never let another person hurt us again, never risk ourselves in relationship again, always play it safe, and always protect our hearts at all costs.

The problem with vows, however, is that they keep us in bondage to the lies the Impostor continually whispers in our ear—things like:

- You're flawed.

- Something is wrong with you. You must hide the real you.

- You can't trust others.

- No one will be there for you because you're not worth it.

- If you don't succeed, no one will like you.

To protect our hearts, we make vows like these:

- I won't let anyone too close.
- I won't trust anyone.
- I have to succeed at all costs or I'm nothing.
- I'll be the best at _____ to prove I'm OK.
- I won't ever give my heart away.
- I'll build a walls around my heart.

Jesse didn't need to be someone famous or do something extraordinary to be significant—she was significant because of what Christ said about her—but she grew up learning to walk on eggshells to protect herself from her dad's outbursts. When he was in one of his moods, she knew the drill: stay away and don't upset the apple cart. She learned to find solace in starving herself. That was one thing no one could control but her. That was one way she could have a voice.

Jesse didn't realize it at the time, but throughout her life she had worshipped the idol of looking good. She had put her trust in a false god—a god that had no power to rescue her.

A SNAKE IN THE GARDEN

To trace the origins of shame, let's go back to the garden and see how the serpent used it to assault Eve's heart. It was the ultimate form of trickery, and she bought into it hook, line, and sinker. Remember the goal was to convince her of her inadequacy and to fill her heart with fear and doubt. If she was lacking something, if she was "less than," if she couldn't trust God, whom could she depend on?

Fear of physical harm is terrifying, but just as paralyzing are the messages we get that shame us into feeling and believing we are nothing. These thoughts—and the beliefs they create—exert tremendous doubt in our hearts about our value and worth. For Eve, it was the first time she had ever experienced these distressing emotions of insecurity and inadequacy ("Maybe God doesn't really care about me"). The serpent then went to work shaming her.

For Jesse, shame was a common occurrence. Remember, when the fear response is activated, our prefrontal cortex (reasoning center) gets bypassed in favor of our amygdala (emotional center), and the danger signal goes off while our rational mind goes to Mars.

How many of us have experienced a condemning tone, a harsh glare, or piercing words of shame that stir up our right-brain activity, making us feel worthless and unlovable? Follow that up with left-brain logic: "You're lacking something. God doesn't care. You aren't worth it."

Eve had her emotional center and her rational mind offering up suggestions to her will. What would she chose to believe? How would she chose to cope? Convinced God didn't really want to know her and couldn't possibly love her, the likely outcome was to turn to her flesh.

Dr. Curt Thompson says this about Eve's dilemma in his book *Anatomy of the Soul*:

> Eve chooses "knowledge" over life. Object over relationship. She acts out of the state of a disintegrated mind, her left and right modes vacillating back and forth, each vying for contentious rule of her destiny. At times she is overrun by the lower and right mode's emotion of fear and shame. To cope with this she shuts them off, deferring to her logical, linear left-mode processing that dismisses her emotion in order to keep her from being overwhelmed by it.[1]

The interesting thing is that Eve made a judgment about her relationship with God based solely on what the serpent told her. She never asked God about it. She didn't seek Him out. She didn't have a conversation with Him. She didn't tell Him she was struggling, and she didn't get His counsel on the matter. She jumped to a conclusion without a shred of evidence to support her beliefs.

Ring a bell? Isn't that what we do? We stop praying. Stop fellowshipping. Stop believing truth. Make wrong assumptions and stop following closely after God. The results are isolation, greater doubt, more fear, and more irrational thoughts.

Why am I belaboring Eve's encounter in the garden? Let's look at Paul's words to see:

> But I am afraid that just as *Eve was deceived by the serpent's cunning, your minds may somehow be*

led astray from your sincere and pure devotion to
Christ.

—2 CORINTHIANS 11:3, EMPHASIS ADDED

Eve's rational mind was deceived like ours. Shame
took advantage of her left-brain capacity for assessing
a situation and drawing a sound conclusion. (Have you
ever drawn an irrational conclusion?) She then dismisses
her feelings (because they are too uncomfortable to deal
with), and she analyzes, makes a judgment call, and
decides some perilous things about herself and about
God. She sells Him out for a piece of fruit.

Thompson goes on to say this about the fallout in the
garden:

> She eats a piece of fruit, supplanting the dynamic,
> life-breathing experience of being known by God,
> the one who mentalizes her perfectly and longs
> to be known by her, with the static, nonrelational,
> temporal creation of her own mind. In rejecting
> this perfect relationship with God, she buys the
> right to acquisition, to forever working to obtain
> and hoard enough so that she will eventually be
> enough. Instead of finding abundance and joy in
> being known, she states her claim on disconnec-
> tion. The rupture is complete.[2]

Satan's schemes are still as alive and evident today as
they were for Eve. He is cunning. His job is to lead us
astray, far from the true heart of God. Take the hook,
believe the lie, do the dirty deed, and experience the
consequences—alone.

How are you being led astray from pure and simple devotion to Christ today? Is there something buried somewhere deep within the recesses of your soul that shames you? What has the cost been to your own sense of self? What has been the cost to your relationship with God? To others?

God Is Always Moving

When we read about the account in the Garden of Eden after Eve and Adam sinned, we often miss a very important point that tells us a lot about the nature and character of God. In Genesis 3:8 we read that when the Lord God was walking in the garden in the cool of the day, He was looking for the man and his wife. God already knew what the deal was with Adam and Eve. It wasn't some big surprise to Him that they sinned. He called to them. He asked, "Where are you?"

Why do you think He did that? He knew where they were—remember, He's God. He knew they were hiding because of their shame.

What we might miss if we aren't paying close attention is that the Lord God was *searching* for them. The New Oxford American Dictionary defines the word *searching* as "trying to find something by looking or otherwise seeking carefully and thoroughly." God was moving toward Adam and Eve. He was in pursuit of them. I believe He was searching for them, not to scold them, not to condemn them, but just to talk to them.

Seem silly—God wanting to talk? Not if you consider

He is a relational God by nature. Not if you think about attachment. God is a pursuer. Relationship is everything to Him. The fact that He is moving toward them is significant for us because what is the first thing we assume when we've done something wrong? Here are a few possibilities you might recognize:

- God is angry with me.

- God will punish me.

- God can never forgive me.

- God doesn't want to have anything to do with me.

- What I've done or who I am repulses the heart of God.

- God doesn't love me.

What's the result of these beliefs? We withdraw from God. We look to the masks to help us cope, and we depend solely on ourselves.

When God went looking for Adam and Eve, He did so with a tender heart. He didn't blast them. He gave them the opportunity to dialogue with Him about the condition of their hearts—but they chose to play the blame game: Adam blames God and Eve ("the woman you gave me"), and Eve blames the serpent ("the serpent deceived me, and I ate"). In that moment they forfeit being known. Thus begins the cycle of hiding.

What are you hiding today? What kind of shame are

you carrying? Surprisingly, there isn't a one-size-fits-all shame category. There are different faces to shame. Let's have a look.

The Many Faces of Shame

Jesse had "try harder" coping strategies because of a belief system that told her she didn't measure up. Whether it was failing to score a goal in a soccer tournament, not getting into an Ivy League college, not becoming the next Miss America, or blaming herself for her sexual abuse, she dealt consistently with performance-based shame.

Performance-based shame

This is the type of shame that would include things we did or failed to do in our lives. For example, the husband who cheats on his wife and feels remorse experiences shame that he did not perform well as a husband. He did something bad. He failed to be a good husband. The kid who fails to live up to performance standards—maybe unrealistic—set by his parents feels shame for not measuring up. These examples suggest that not only did we perform poorly in what we did or failed to do, but also we have now *become someone* who is a failure.

This type of shame comes in the form of regrets and "if onlys" that haunt our hearts and minds. "If only I hadn't cheated, my wife wouldn't have left me." "If only I hadn't pushed so hard, my child wouldn't have committed suicide." "If only I had gotten better grades, my parents would have been proud of me." "If only..."

Performance-based shame has deep roots that anchor

themselves to our souls and tell us the problem isn't just that we *made* mistake but that we *are* a mistake.

Generational shame

Kelly's father was an alcoholic. She grew up never wanting to invite friends over for fear that her dad would act inappropriately. She was terrified that if she married, her husband would become an alcoholic. Because of the generational shame she carried, Kelly didn't trust men, and she never married.

Mary struggled with a drug problem her entire adult life. She was in and out of treatment centers and caused her family a great deal of heartache and shame. Her children felt labeled in school because of her illness.

Bill was an older black man who remembers the days when racial prejudice was rampant. He was continually marginalized, and it radically impacted his self-esteem. He passed his feelings and beliefs down to his children.

Sam cheated on his wife, Carla, with her best friend. Carla can't trust anyone anymore.

David's father committed adultery. His mother divorced him. David bears the stigma of his parents' divorce, fearing he'll repeat the same patterns in his own life. To protect himself, he stays clear of commitment.

All these scenarios foster a deep sense of shame not only for those involved but also for future generations. The Bible calls this generational sin. And while we can break the strongholds of generational curses, they do leave scars on those we love.

Image-bearing shame

When we put forth our authentic self and it is publicly shamed—remember the incident Jesse had on the soccer field?—it can cause us to build walls. If our authentic self isn't good enough, we'll make sure the Impostor is.

While performance-based shame deals with our behavior, image-bearing shame deals with our perception of how others view us. To reduce our anxiety, we will often wear the mask of pleasing so that other people won't reject us. Jesse felt disappointment in herself for not meeting the imposed standards of others, but her disappointment in herself for not living up to her own standards solidified her belief that she was a failure.

Victim shame

Jesse suffered sexual abuse and believed somehow it was her fault. This is not an uncommon belief for children, but that belief sent her on a downward spiral of self-destructive activity. Besides the eating disorder, she also had a past history of engaging in self-injurious behavior, cutting herself to numb the pain. Her beliefs about not being able to stop these behaviors kept her stuck in victim mode and reinforced her already established beliefs about her weakness.

Jesse was a victim of abuse, but to heal, she couldn't stay there. She had to tell the story of her abuse in order to get out from behind the shame.

Being a victim of sexual abuse or being in an abusive relationship where we are constantly being shamed can destroy our hearts. We must never discount that, but looking to the idols of the world—be they body image, weight, appearance, career, success, or whatever else we prize to fill ourselves—reveals the real tragedy: we are not victims; we are idolaters.

Dan Allender says this in his book *Cry of the Soul*:

> In idolatrous worship, we are exalting self-sufficiency and self-determining power. An idol is really nothing more than an object or idea or desire that allows the creator to worship himself. Shame arises when worship—the ascribing of glory and honor—is invested in self rather than in God.[3]

Body shame

Most people struggle with body image issues. (If you need proof, just ask any woman who looks into a mirror or visit a local gym.) But body shame goes a lot deeper than complaining that you're fat or out of shape. This type of shame means you loathe your body, and it can be the result of being sexually abused. To avoid the feelings of being sexually vulnerable, a woman might gain weight as a way of hiding her physical self. She might purposely try to look unattractive or unfeminine. She might starve herself in an attempt to dewomanize herself.

Body shame carries with it a whole host of lies such as: "If I were skinny, my life would be better." "If I'm thin, I will have my partner's love and approval." Body shame may also keep you isolated. You may notice you're avoiding going out or being with friends because you feel unattractive. All of these fears and beliefs keep you feeling anxious and ashamed of who you are.

To recover, you have to be willing to modify the existing beliefs you hold about your shape and size being the sole cause for your misery. Challenging the veracity of these beliefs includes looking at them realistically. If you've ever been thin enough, ask yourself if you were really happy and fulfilled. For Jesse, the answer was no. It didn't matter how thin she was, she was still insecure. The path to healing requires seeing yourself as Christ sees you, remembering your body is the temple of the Holy Spirit:

> Do you not know that your body is a temple of the Holy Spirit, who is in you, whom you have received from God? You are not your own: you were bought at a price. Therefore honor God with your body.
> —1 CORINTHIANS 6:19–20

OUR SACRED VOW

Matt was only six years old. He wanted to surprise his dad and wash the car for him. When his father got home from work, Matt's mom told him to come outside and look at what Matt had done. His father carefully walked around the car, surveying the job his small son had done. With one finger, he swiped the rear wheel of the car, revealing some dirt Matt had missed. Looking at his son, he said, "Never send a boy to do a man's job."

Matt was devastated. Shamed by his father's remarks, his young mind made a vow: "I will never let anyone hurt me like that again. I'll show you. I'll wall off my heart, and I won't trust."

A vow is a solemn promise that sets into motion a course of action. Vows that are made to protect our hearts wall us off from the one thing we were created for: being known. Vows are the result of a real or perceived loss. If they aren't aligned to the purposes of God, they can have perilous effects on our hearts. Survey the list below, and ask yourself if any of these vows apply to your life:

- I will never give away my heart.

- I will always be in control.

- I will never trust another person.

- I will never be vulnerable.

- I will appear perfect.

- I will be successful to prove something to others.

- I will pretend so no one will see my real feelings.

- I will never forgive.

- I'll never let anyone close. I'll do whatever I have to and prove them wrong.

It doesn't matter how much we succeed in life—our hearts still battle the silent scream of shame echoing deep from within the recesses of our souls that tells us we're flawed, that we're not good enough, that we can't cut it. It's us trying to do something—*anything*—that will make us worthy of feeling the love we so desperately desire. It's why Adam and Eve covered themselves with the fig leaves—it was something to do to try and hide the shame that threatened to overwhelm them.

What things have you looked to in order to silence the scream of your soul? Stop right now and ask yourself: Has it really worked? If not, you have to be willing to lay it down. You have to give up on the beliefs behind the vows that have driven your life away from dependence on God and instead be willing to surrender the control of your life to the only One who can fill you.

Jesse made several vows throughout her life. They all boiled down to one core belief that said she must protect her heart at any cost. In so doing, she placed herself on the throne as God. She took over the job of the Holy Spirit. It cost her in all areas of her life. As we surveyed her life and the effects of her vows, we saw the following results:

- She held others on the periphery of her life.

- She was the consummate pleaser.

- She was terrified of rejection.

- She took no risks in relationships.

- She was never truly known by another person.

- She had abandonment issues.

- She was controlling.
- She constantly needed to achieve for approval.
- She couldn't accept failure.

Jesse was tired of trying to measure up. She was tired of free-falling. She was tired of doing it all on her own and in her way. She was ready to enter into the temple of the Lord to find rest and peace for her soul. She was ready to be hid in the shelter of His tabernacle and to be covered under His wings. She was ready to wait on the Lord.

LIVING PROOF

Shame is a killer. It assaults our identity. It robs us from intimacy with God because we believe we are unworthy to come before the throne of grace. The very thing we need to heal a heart that's hemorrhaging lies beyond our grasp: relationship. Buying into the idea that we have to clean ourselves up before we can come to God, we allow the enemy of our souls to rob us of the inheritance that's ours to claim.

The problem is, most people don't even realize shame is at the core of their low self-esteem. Look around you. The person sitting next to you at church could have been abused. Could have been an addict. Could have been betrayed. Could have had an abortion. Or maybe it's not something so dramatic. Maybe they had a dad who told them they'd never measure up. Maybe their mom walked out. Maybe they got bullied in school. Underneath it all is shame—the core belief that we're *nothing*.

The truth is that to heal from the shame that threatens to undo us, we need relationship, relationship with the only One who can heal us from shame's deadly grasp. He gave us living proof of our worth, and He died to prove it. He emptied Himself. He relinquished all His rights as God and clothed Himself in humility and lowliness to make a way back for us in the midst of our brokenness. He did it so we would know just how much He cares about our hearts and how much He longs to lead us into His loving arms.

All it takes is for the living God to whisper your name. All it takes is for you to allow Him to come near despite the agony of your shame. All it takes is for you to listen as He calls you home—home, where you're safe. Just as the prodigal's father ran to meet his son, overjoyed that he had come home, so God our Father runs to greet us and welcome us back into His loving care.

Benny Hester describes this beautifully in his song "When God Ran." He recounts the journey of when the prodigal son left home and how he broke his Father's heart. He believed the lie that things could never be the same between him and God because of what he had done. Then, one night, something happened. The God of the universe reached down and made Himself known to the broken prodigal. Who knows, He could have used a word, a circumstance, or a person who revealed the time-less message: God doesn't just take a casual walk after us when we've lost our way—He runs to us, takes us in His loving arms, and assures us that no matter what we've done, no matter how bad we've blown it, He still loves us with an unfailing love. This is the truth that led him back to the arms of the Father.

Beloved, you are totally acceptable in God's sight. His desire is that you draw near to Him. He wants you to know that the great exchange His Son made on the cross changed everything. Here is the evidence to prove it:

> While we were enemies we were reconciled to God.
> —ROMANS 5:10, NAS

> There is now no condemnation for those who are in Christ Jesus.
> —ROMANS 8:1

> Having canceled the charge of our legal indebtedness, which stood against us and condemned us; he has taken it away, nailing it to the cross.
> —COLOSSIANS 2:14

> For we know that our old self was crucified with him so that the body ruled by sin might be done away with, that we should no longer be slaves to sin.
> —ROMANS 6:6

> But now he has reconciled you by Christ's physical body through death to present you holy in his sight, without blemish and free from accusation.
> —COLOSSIANS 1:22

> It is finished.
> —JOHN 19:30

These verses are living proof that we are new creations in Him!

It's Time to Begin

But before we can start the rebuilding process in our lives, before we can risk being known in relationship, we have to deal with our shame. We have to be willing to take off the masks we've worn and expose ourselves. We have to allow God entrance to the interior of our hearts to do what only He can do: set us free.

For Jesse to break out of the shame she felt about who she was, for her to give up on the "try harder" life and start the rebuilding process, she would have to fight the battle for her heart daily, and she would have to be convinced that she was worth being known by God.

The battle would bring trouble. Battles always do. They always require something of us. But I assured Jesse that the same God who searched for Adam and Eve in the garden was searching for her. He wanted her to be found, He wanted her to be known, and He wanted to be known by her. All that would be required for now was a willingness to open her heart and receive. Together, we would start the rebuilding process.

> "You will seek me and find me when you seek me with all your heart. I will be found by you," declares the LORD.
> —JEREMIAH 29:13–14

CONSIDER THIS

- What were your earliest recollections of being shamed? How did you cope with those experiences? What do you think they did to your heart?

- What types of shame did you experience?

- How has carrying shame affected your relationship with others? With God?

- Have you ever made a vow? What beliefs lay underneath that vow? What effect did it have on your life?

- How does the idea of God searching for you affect you?

Chapter 10
REBUILDING THE WALLS

Your people will rebuild the ancient ruins and will raise up the age-old foundations; you will be called Repairer of Broken Walls, Restorer of Streets with Dwellings.
—ISAIAH 58:12

THROUGHOUT OUR JOURNEY together thus far we've learned from Jesse, and we've learned from Adam and Eve. But what might other biblical characters have to teach us?

I'm so glad you asked, as there just happens to be a gold mine of goodness in the Scriptures when it comes to the Impostor's effect on the people of God. For starters, take Nehemiah. Things were going downhill fast in Jerusalem in 445 BC, and Nehemiah was sorely grieved. The wall in Jerusalem was broken down, and the gate was in ruins. In the month of Nisan in the twentieth year of King Artaxerxes, Nehemiah was the cup-bearer to the king. One day, as he brought the king his wine, Nehemiah's face looked so downcast that the king thought he was ill. He inquired of Nehemiah, "Why does your face look so sad when you are not ill? This can be nothing but sadness of heart" (Neh. 2:2). It was then that Nehemiah made his petition to the great king and asked if he could return to Jerusalem and rebuild his city. Here is their discourse:

> I was very much afraid, but I said to the king, "May the king live forever! Why should my face not look sad when the city where my ancestors are buried lies in ruins, and its gates have been destroyed by fire?" The king said to me, "What is it you want?"
>
> Then I prayed to the God of heaven, and I answered the king, "If it pleases the king and if your servant has found favor in his sight, let him send me to the city in Judah where my ancestors are buried so that I can rebuild it."
>
> —Nehemiah 2:2–5

Here's what we notice about Nehemiah:

- He was *sad* because the city of Jerusalem lay in ruins.

- He was *afraid*, but he took a risk.

- He *prayed* to God to give him wisdom.

- He *confessed* his sin and the sin of his people.

- He *asked*—took action—for what he needed from the king.

- He faced great *obstacles*.

- He was *willing*—surrendered—to facing obstacles.

- He kept hope *alive.*

- He *received* what God had promised.

Just like you and me, Nehemiah faced a dark night of the soul. He was downcast when he learned the news of the current state of Jerusalem and his fellow countrymen. The Chaldeans had left the city in ruins, and the inhabitants were living in poverty, fear, and slavery. They were very vulnerable to other attacks by surrounding enemies. When Hanani brought the news to Nehemiah about the condition of Jerusalem, Nehemiah wept and mourned for days:

> They said to me, "Those who survived the exile and are back in the province are in great trouble and disgrace. The wall of Jerusalem is broken down, and its gates have been burned with fire."
> —NEHEMIAH 1:3

Nehemiah was grieved in spirit because his people's lives were in ruins, but note: Nehemiah dealt with his grief by pouring out his complaint to God. What do we learn from this? That we must entreat God in our time of need, being confident of His grace and mercy toward us, knowing He will provide what is needed moment by moment.

Nehemiah was afraid, but right in the middle of his fear he sought God. He was afraid of how the king would respond to his grief because in his day, one did not bother the king with personal problems—ever. He was also concerned about how the king would respond to his request to go to Jerusalem. If he incurred the king's wrath, if he even misplaced a word in his petition, it could have resulted in his losing the king's favor. Nehemiah chose not to let his fear get the best of him. He didn't succumb to self-pity or shrink back from the enormity of his fear. He came boldly before the throne of grace and cast all his anxieties on the God of heaven and earth.

Nehemiah prayed, but he didn't stop there. He decided to take action by taking a risk and asking the king for what he needed. He desired to rebuild the walls of Jerusalem, but he knew it would take more than his strength to do so. He knew he would encounter great obstacles as he set out to rebuild the walls, but here's the key: It didn't stop him. Nothing would stop him because he was fighting a battle he was passionate about. That didn't mean he didn't struggle. It didn't mean he didn't lose heart or get discouraged—he did. But he chose to trust God despite everything coming against him.

There will always be obstacles in our way when we decide to risk. That's a given. In Nehemiah 4 we see he faces tremendous opposition in the rebuilding process. As we try and recover from the damage, hurt, and ruin we have incurred in life, the enemy seeks to thwart our recovery through discouragement, ridicule, and rejection. Here's what Nehemiah was facing in the opening of chapter 4:

> When Sanballat heard that we were rebuilding the wall, he became angry and was greatly incensed. He ridiculed the Jews, and in the presence of his

associates and the army of Samaria, he said, "What are those feeble Jews doing? Will they restore their wall? Will they offer sacrifices? Will they finish in a day? Can they bring the stones back to life from those heaps of rubble—burned as they are?" Tobiah the Ammonite, who was at his side, said, "What they are building—even a fox climbing up on it would break down their wall of stones!"

—NEHEMIAH 4:1–3

For Jesse, the voice of her eating disorder posed a great obstacle to her rebuilding process. She was afraid it would try to creep back into her life and undo her progress. But I asked her to consider how she could use that fear to keep her dependent on God. Some days would be hard. Some days she would feel as if she was falling backward. But I asked if she could consider the fact that victory wasn't necessarily a set of desired outcomes. Victory was a person—the Lord Jesus Christ, in fact—and if she could keep her focus on Him, not on herself, she wouldn't measure victory in terms of outcomes any longer. It wouldn't be about what she ate or didn't eat; it would be about who she depended on when she was faced with that choice.

The next thing we notice about Nehemiah was that he confessed his sin and the sin of Israel. In his confession he humbled himself and took on the shame of his people. Nehemiah is fervent in his pleas for mercy, and he is ready to accept the discipline of God on his people, but he appeals to the promises God made to his forefathers.

He places his hope in the unfailing love and mercy of God and the covenant He made with Israel:

> Remember your word to your servant, for you have given me hope. My comfort in my suffering is this: Your promise preserves my life.
>
> —PSALM 119:49

Nehemiah was surrendered to the will of God. The forces coming against him were roused, as we see in Nehemiah 2:10: "When Sanballat the Horonite and Tobiah the Ammonite official heard about this, they were very much disturbed that someone had come to promote the welfare of the Israelites." In spite of the difficulties that lay ahead of him, Nehemiah was willing to surrender his rights for things to go smoothly and for him to be understood by those who opposed him. He was willing to experience feeling scared, inadequate, misunderstood, and insecure. The moment you and I are not willing to surrender our rights to whatever it is we fear, we forfeit our souls to dependency on the flesh.

In the end, Nehemiah prevailed against the enemies who would have obstructed his cause and laughed him out of what he was trying to accomplish. He could have easily lost hope. The city was a mess, and not all the Israelites were on board to help him. When he looked at the desolations of the walls and saw the enormity of the task before him, I'm certain it was easy to lose heart. But he didn't stay caught up in his discouragement. He continually pressed forward and encouraged his countrymen to rise up and build.

Finally, Nehemiah prayed that God would prosper him in his undertaking and give him favor. Favor was granted, and it changed the course of history. Let us not discount the power of prayer as we walk through adversity. Let us remind our heavenly Father of His promises to us, and let us speak them out with boldness, as these verses remind us:

> The LORD is trustworthy in all he promises and faithful in all he does.
> —PSALM 145:13

> No matter how many promises God has made, they are "Yes" in Christ. And so through him the "Amen" is spoken by us to the glory of God.
> —2 CORINTHIANS 1:20

> Your promise preserves my life.
> —PSALM 119:50

> May your unfailing love be my comfort, according to your promise to your servant.
> —PSALM 119:76

WRESTLING MATCH

Much like Jacob and Job, Nehemiah wrestled with God and prevailed. He wept, wailed, fasted, and prayed, and he reminded God of His former goodness to His people. All throughout the Bible, in fact, we see the characters in every story ranted, raved, and struggled, and through their struggles something powerful happened: they found God.

177

This is the journey set before all of us—to question, wrestle, fight, and decide about the heart of God. Only then can the process of rebuilding begin to take shape, because to rebuild on solid ground requires the foundation to be secure. In order for that to happen, it must be built on solid rock.

Why does it have to happen this way? Why must we struggle and suffer and walk after our own ways to finally realize in the end we really can't control anything? Because nothing gets our attention like suffering. It brings us face-to-face with our own inadequacy, which in turn reveals to us the inexhaustible sufficiency of Christ.

Jesse wrestled with the Almighty. She did what Nehemiah did, and God prevailed. She expressed her sadness through the telling of her narrative. She grieved her losses and put words to her pain. She prayed, confessed, and asked her heavenly Father for what she needed. She surrendered her eating disorder and all the ways she had walked after her flesh to make life work. For the first time in years she actually had hope. Now she was ready to receive from God.

That was when I noticed a shift in her. Something was different. I knew Jesse had *experienced* God. She had moved from an intellectual knowing of Him to an encounter with Him, and once that happened, I knew she would be OK. Sometimes it's a verse of Scripture we read. Sometimes it's something someone else says. It doesn't really matter how God does it; He just makes something *rhema* to us, and boom—it's done. We're changed forever.

Wrestling calls us to make a choice—a choice about our hearts and what will become of them. Jesse made the decision to pick up the shattered pieces of her heart and risk stepping out to begin the process of rebuilding her life. She had a lot of truth at this point in our walk together. So the first thing I wanted to know was this: Could she call forth desire from the distant corners of her soul and coauthor a new story for her life with God?

THE INNER WELL

When an architect thinks about building, the first thing he does is to draw up some ideas. He allows the ideas that are birthed in his mind to come forth on paper. To do that, he has to draw on his creativity and passion. He has to draw from what is as common to him as breathing: creating. The passion for his craft is the fuel that acts like a strong current running deep within him. He cannot *not* create. He cannot *not* tap into that which comes forth with passion from his soul. He cannot *not* draw from the wellspring of creative life that resides within him.

As believers, the life of God flows through our hearts and souls, so we must first and foremost draw on that inner strength of Christ to propel us forward in our rebuilding. This inner life, the one we possess and can draw from daily, gives us strength and purpose. When we chose to draw from the living water, passion is aroused and awakens that which may have lain dormant for years. When we draw from this living water, when we

IMPOSTOR

are confident it has no end, we can embrace security in the love of God and be freed up to live purposeful lives.

Often we don't know how to really access this inner life. We may read our Bibles, go to church, and offer up heart-felt prayers, but if we're really honest, God still seems a bit distant. So the question to consider for now is this: What are you doing to facilitate the emergence of God's life within you? Because the truth is, you can't draw forth something you haven't nurtured and grown up.

The rebuilding phase of life requires that we draw on the help, counsel, wisdom, and availability of others. If by now we're convinced God created us for relation-ship, then we should be convinced we can't go it alone. Community is necessary to draw strength for the journey ahead. It will help to lay the secure foundation when our journey becomes too wearisome.

A Secure Foundation

The men of Nehemiah's day had to survey the damage done to the walls. They had to focus on what needed ref-ormation and what could stand as it was.

Part of their task was to check the foundation of the walls to see if they were secure. A foundation serves as the lowest load-bearing part of a building. It is typically underground and carries the weight of everything that lies above it. If the foundation is secure, all is well.

Jesus thinks the foundations we build on are pretty important. That's why He tells us not to build a house on shifting sand:

180

> Therefore everyone who hears these words of mine
> and puts them into practice is like a wise man who
> built his house on the rock. The rain came down,
> the streams rose, and the winds blew and beat
> against that house; yet it did not fall, because it
> had its foundation on the rock. But everyone who
> hears these words of mine and does not put them
> into practice is like a foolish man who built his
> house on sand. The rain came down, the streams
> rose, and the winds blew and beat against that
> house, and it fell with a great crash.
>
> —MATTHEW 7:24

To check the pulse on Jesse's heart, I presented her with a task: survey the damage in her life that was caused by having built on a shaky foundation. I wanted her to look at all the false beliefs, lies, and unhealthy behaviors and decide what needed to go so she could rebuild on a sure foundation. She readily made a list.

Next, I asked her to think about what truly authentic parts of herself would stay. By this time the eating disorder had lost the majority of its control over her thought life. She knew the voice of God was stronger than the former lies she had readily played over and over in her head. She was also done with all the pleasing and trying to measure up stuff. She was totally convinced it was a dead end.

Jesse realized that underneath the Impostor's mask, she was really a kind person. She recognized her gifts of mercy and compassion. She realized she wasn't weak at all—the truth was she was anything but. God had been there all along, trying to get her attention, trying to show her the only thing that was weak was what she had put her trust in. She realized the strength she now possessed wasn't her own, that He was there all along, providing what was needed to lead her to the high places. She had just been too afraid to let Him in.

Jesse was finally able to see it had taken tremendous courage to face her issues. It had taken perseverance to keep going when everything inside her wanted to quit. It had taken faith to risk. It had taken a willingness to surrender her fears and choose to trust. Wearing the mask was the easy way out.

She now had a firm foundation, and she was ready to start thinking about resurrecting desire from the distant corners of her soul.

The Resurrection of Desire

Nehemiah had a dream to rebuild the foundations that were destroyed. He faced tremendous opposition and discouragement from the forces of evil. It took courage and commitment to press on. I told Jesse to expect no less, as the enemy of her soul would call forth all the fury of hell to pull her back into the pit of despair. She must be on alert and engaged for the battle that was being waged against her heart. With that in mind, we set out to explore the desires of her heart.

Desire is a powerful force. It's a strong feeling of want that propels the human soul to action. It's the stuff that romance novels, movies, and story are made of. It was placed into the heart of man by the hand of God. God desired to create. God desired to love. God desired to give man the desires of his heart because of God's great pleasure. Take a look:

> He will give you the desires of your heart.
>
> —PSALM 37:4

> Who satisfies your desires with good things.
>
> —PSALM 103:5

> You open your hand and satisfy the desires of every living thing.
>
> —PSALM 145:16

> What a person desires is unfailing love.
>
> —PROVERBS 19:22

If God is the author of desire, then what does He want us to do with it? We know all too well that it can be used for evil as well as good. The answer seems obvious: unpack your desires and live them out according to God's will. But before that can happen—before we can move toward desire—we have to take into account what killed it in the first place.

For Jesse, the continual disappointments of life, the abuse, the eating disorder, the lack of secure connection—all these things shut her heart down to desire. She got used to living half-dead.

Maybe you aren't sure exactly when you lost heart. Maybe you can't remember what one event or series of events were responsible for breaking your heart, but somewhere along the line you decided to abandon desire. The secret for Jesse—for all of us—is to allow God to take us back to the place of desire and connect us once again to our own hearts. If God is the author of desire, we must meet with Him and allow Him to do the work of rekindling our desire according to *His* will. Only then will it flow from us as naturally as it does for the wall builder.

> Your people will rebuild the ancient ruins and will raise up the age-old foundations; you will be called Repairer of Broken Walls, Restorer of Streets with Dwellings.
>
> —ISAIAH 58:12

John Eldredge reminds us our response to the call of faith is centered in desire. He says this in his compelling book *The Journey of Desire:*

> At its core, Christianity begins with an invitation to desire. Look at the way Jesus relates to people. As he did with the fellow at the Sheep Gate, he is continually taking them into their hearts, to their deepest desires.[1]

What begins for us as an invitation to desire gets twisted into a performance-based religion that can give no life. We begin our journey of faith by receiving the free gift of salvation, and somewhere along the way we make it about what we're doing to get God to like us a little better. Eldredge goes on:

The Jews of his [Jesus's] day were practicing a very soul-killing spirituality, a lifeless religion of duty and obligation. They had abandoned desire and replaced it with knowledge and performance as the key to life. The synagogue was the place to go and learn how to get with the program. Desire was out of the question; duty was the path that people must walk. No wondered they feared Jesus.[2]

Jesus spoke a different kind of message. He spoke about the heart. He knew the law would never satisfy. Rules and regulations rarely do. He knew if we put our hope or trust in the law, it would eventually shut our hearts down to life. And life is all we need. It's really the heart of what we're after. It will only be found in the life of Christ.

He who has the Son has life.

—1 JOHN 5:12, NKJV

I have come that they may have life.

—JOHN 10:10, NKJV

The Spirit gives life; the flesh counts for nothing. The words I have spoken to you—they are full of the Spirit and life.

—JOHN 6:63

You make known to me the path of life; you fill me with joy in your presence, with eternal pleasures at your right hand.

—PSALM 16:11

Jesse spent a lot of years missing life. She spent a lot of years following the rules and wearing the masks, believing somehow they would give her the life she prized. This life will never provide that because Eden was lost. We had to settle for a substitute, but God devised a plan—a plan of redemption. That's what the story is really all about: redemption. It's the story God is telling, and He's using Jesse's story, your story, and my story to complete the narrative. As each of our stories unfolds, God is saying—no, He's shouting, "Enter into the bigger story I'm telling. Step into desire and see what I'll do with it." If we don't enter in, our hearts will be lost.

Eldredge says this about the *Return of the Prodigal Son* painting by Rembrandt:

> In the painting, the elder brother stands a step *above* the reunion of father and son. He will not step down, enter in. He is above it all. But who receives redemption? The scandalous message of the story is this: those who kill desire—the legalists, the dutiful—are not the ones who experience the father's embrace. The question is not, Dare we desire, but dare we *not* desire.[3]

The point is this: The younger brother wasn't afraid to enter in. He wasn't afraid to risk. He wasn't afraid to ask for forgiveness. He wasn't afraid to tell his story. He wasn't afraid to live from his heart. He wasn't afraid of his desires. In the end, he was the one who found real freedom.

THE DECLARATION OF DESIRE

Here's another story I'll share with you about desire, and it's the story of Bartimaeus. Bartimaeus was a man who lived in the wilderness for many years. Blind since birth, he desired to see—so much so that his boldness caught the ear of the Savior. Bartimaeus made his desire known by shouting out to Jesus in a loud voice. The disciples seemed annoyed, but Jesus stopped. He heard. He listened. He acted.

The next thing Scripture tells us is that Bartimaeus cast off his cloak: "Throwing aside his cloak, he jumped up and came to Jesus" (Mark 10:50, NAS). This is important because, like the widow who gave her last coin, this was probably the only thing Bartimaeus owned, and he was willing to cast it off to come to Christ—naked and unashamed. God will never despise a broken and contrite heart. We must come stripped of all pretense and self-sufficiency. He wants us to remove the masks we've worn in the name of having it all together, and to come instead with excitement and expectancy, just as Bartimaeus displayed.

Then Jesus asks Bartimaeus what may seem like a strange question: "What do you want Me to do for you?" Didn't He know? Yes, He did. But that question required Bartimaeus to notice some things about his condition— physically, emotionally, and spiritually. That's what Jesus was after. He wanted Bartimaeus to voice his desire. He brings Bartimaeus face-to-face with it by asking the question. Bartimaeus says, "Rabboni, I want [desire] to regain my sight" (v. 51, NAS).

We can learn a lot from this story. Jesus encouraged Bartimaeus to hope—and hope is central to the gospel. It's also what keeps the heart alive when the bottom drops out of our lives. Bartimaeus hoped in Jesus, and he believed he would find mercy and healing. Isn't that what we all desire? "Jesus, Son of David, have mercy on me" (v. 47, NAS).

What we see next is classic Jesus. He brings Bartimaeus *near.* He meets his gaze and listens to his lament. Remember attunement from attachment theory? It tells us that when we have the secure and compassionate presence of another, healing occurs.

Jesus knew Bartimaeus had a longing to be made whole. No greater pleasure does the Savior have than to fulfill our desires and longings as we come to Him as a child comes to a loving father. You may not be blind, but if you have a need, Jesus is asking you the same thing He asked Bartimaeus: "What do you want Me to do for you?"

The final thing we notice from this passage is that once he was healed, Bartimaeus was changed. His encounter with his Lord left him different. It changed his heart. It birthed a desire in him. We aren't told much about what happened to Bartimaeus after his healing, but we do know "he began following Him on the road" (v. 52, NAS).

Whether you are in the middle of a crisis, at the end of a crisis, or anticipating one, stop and ask yourself the same question I asked Jesse: "What do you want Jesus to do for you?" How will you use your answer to move forward with God?

REBUILDING THE RUINS

Having laid a firm foundation and resurrected our desire, it's now time to truly rebuild. The apostle Peter describes some important things we should consider as we reconstruct our walls:

> Make every effort to add to your faith goodness; and to goodness, knowledge; and to knowledge, self-control; and to self-control, perseverance; and to perseverance, godliness; and to godliness, mutual affection; and to mutual affection, love.
> —2 PETER 1:5–7

When these qualities become the brick and mortar in our building, we reconstruct the walls and gates of our lives with authenticity.

Nehemiah's rebuilding process centered around ten gates in Jerusalem. The late Bible teacher Ray Stedman outlined the significance of each of the gates in a fantastic teaching on Nehemiah. Let's look at the names of a few of them to learn what else is important during the rebuilding phase of our lives.

Sheep Gate

The first gate was the Sheep Gate. This gate symbolized the Lamb of God. This is the gate through which the sheep were brought into the city to be sacrificed at the altar. This gate reveals the principle of the cross and reminds us that not only must the foundation we build on be secure, but our trust in God will also always be required for building strength in our lives.

Fountain Gate

The name of this gate reminds us of the words of the Lord Jesus to the woman at the well in John 4:14: "The water that I shall give [you] will become in [you] a fountain of water springing up into everlasting life" (NKJV). This gate speaks of the Holy Spirit, who is the river of life in us. It is the flow of God's Spirit in our lives that enables us to obey His will and His Word.

Water Gate

Water is a symbol of the Word of God. Stedman observed that the Water Gate did not need to be repaired. It was the only part of the wall still standing. Scripture mentions that people lived near it, but it never says it needed repair. In the same way, the Word of God never breaks down. It never needs to be repaired, only to be reinhabited.

East Gate

Stedman noted: "The East Gate faced the rising sun, and is the gate of hope. It is the gate of anticipation of what is yet to come when all the trials of life and all the struggles of earth will end and the glorious new sun will rise on the new day of God. This gate needs to be rebuilt in many of us who fall under the pessimistic spirit of this age and are crushed by the hopelessness of our time."[4]

Horse Gate

The horse in Scripture is a symbol of warfare or of the need to do battle against the forces of darkness. This is the battle Paul described in Ephesians 6:12: "For we are not contending against flesh and blood, but against the principalities, against the powers, against the world rulers of this present darkness, against the spiritual hosts of wickedness in the heavenly places" (RSV).

Muster Gate

The Muster Gate is literally the "examination gate." It apparently was the place where judgment was conducted. Stedman notes: "This was evidently the place where judgment was conducted. We need to sit and take a look at ourselves every now and then—to stop and reevaluate what we are doing."[5]

Stedman reminds us of a most powerful truth as he concludes:

> The cross must be at the beginning and the end of every life. Undergirding everything is this principle, out of death comes life. Out of the subjection of our natural desires to the will of God comes the life of God filling us full and blessing our hearts.[6]

We can learn from the Book of Nehemiah how to strengthen the walls in our lives. When we don't build up our walls, it's easy for our lives to crumble, but when we put God right in the middle of our lives, when we give Him His rightful purpose, He will restore the broken walls and give us a vision for the future.

Jesse learned a lot about what was necessary for rebuilding. But I still had one more important thing to teach her: how to practice the presence of God. Let's enter in.

Consider This

- The Book of Nehemiah was all about rebuilding. What do you sense God is saying to you about the need to rebuild in your own life?

- What may or may not be hindering you in the rebuilding process?

- Do you relate to blind Bartimaeus? Why or why not?

- What do you want the Lord to do for you at this time?

- What do you sense the Lord wanting you to do with *your* desires?

- Can you relate to any of Ray Stedman's gates? If so, which one(s)?

- How has God restored your broken walls in the past? Can you trust Him now in whatever trial you face to do the same? Why? Why not?

Chapter 11
PRACTICING THE PRESENCE OF GOD

The problem is not entirely in finding the room of one's own, the time alone, difficult and necessary as that is. The problem is more how to still the soul in the midst of its activities.[1]

—ANNE MORROW LINDBERGH,

GIFT FROM THE SEA

M Y HUSBAND CALLED her Bella. It's a middle name that describes my granddaughter's beauty. When she sees me, her world stands still. She runs and jumps into my arms—such joy, such excitement. She delights my soul. Such is the blessing of grandbabies.

As we play, I watch her. Life is simple. She mothers her dollies and her baby sister. She is content. I find myself wishing I could keep the world from moving in and dismantling the joy and contentment of such simple moments in her life. I wonder how I can demonstrate a life that teaches her this discipline in spite of my own wandering heart.

Genuine contentment flows from what I love, and I confess that sometimes I don't love wisely. This little one teaches me that only one thing is necessary for contentment: *presence*—the giving away of the heart to the one you love. I feel it when she reaches for me in the night when she's afraid. She touches my face for assurance. Presence calms her. She asks for her song. I sing. Contentment comes. We're both satisfied because we feel the unspoken love between us. The presence her love brings draws me to *His* love.

This is the love we were created for. It paints a picture on the canvas of our souls and opens our hearts to experience the joy of true contentment. Then the world steps in, and I become aware of all the things that lead me away from the one thing most necessary—presence, *His presence.*

I ask myself why it's so hard for me to remain content in perfect love. My heart is so prone to wandering. I chase after the idols of career, success, relationships, and control, believing somehow they will fill me. I say I desire contentment in Him, but I choose a divided heart. I say I desire His peace, but I allow chaos. I say I desire solitude with Him, but I seldom take the time to be still. Whatever direction I allow desire to take me will determine the condition of my heart. If I choose unwisely, true contentment eludes me.

Then the little one comes and reminds me. She whispers in my ear a secret. We giggle. She reminds me not to concern myself with the duties of the world. We have more important work to do together. She tugs on my hand to suggest the urgency of our mission. "Play," she says and invites me to step into the wonder of contentment that requires only presence.

The sweetness of presence connects us and makes our world together come alive. It's about knowing and being known. It brings me back to the Father, back to the presence that stirs my heart and reminds me He is inviting me, moment by moment, to experience contentment, just as the little one does, tugging at my heart to know and be known in a way no one else can.

Jesus is calling us, beloved. Receive the gift of contentment today through the gift of union and the power of His presence.

THE MYSTERY OF RELATIONSHIP

Over and over we've talked about the social orientation God demonstrates in and through the Trinity, the mystery of three persons in one spirit life. This three-in-one God invites us to be partakers in the greatest of mysteries: union. It is through this union that we are saved, healed, restored, made new, and, perhaps most importantly, *known*. Desire for what we were created for stirs our longings, and we were created to *know* and *be known* by God and by others.

Our longing for relationship proves it. We long for our parents to know us. We long to find that special someone to be a safe haven for us so that we can open our hearts to being known. We long to know and be known by our children, to love and be loved. We desire close friends to care enough to dig below the surface of our pretense. We long to know ourselves as well. And most importantly we long to know that the God of the universe loves us unconditionally. All of it is about intimacy, and intimacy is only possible through the power of union.

Jesse understood what I was talking about related

to this because she realized she had been joined to her Impostor for most of her life. Jenni Schaefer illustrates this too in her book *Life Without Ed* when she talks about her eating disorder as a marriage partner she was unequally yoked to. In order to be free, she had to divorce the Impostor, Ed, and find herself. For Jesse, union meant finding God, because only then would she find her true identity.

In the movie *Chariots of Fire* Eric Liddell says, "When I run, I feel God's pleasure." What did he mean? He meant that when he ran, he was in complete union with God. He experienced God, and from that union desire sprang forth. He drew from something deep within. He ran because he drew from the desire that flowed out of union. John Eldredge and Brent Curtis say this in *The Sacred Romance* about Jesus's union with the Father:

> Jesus ran because he wanted to, not simply because he had to or because the Father told him to. He ran "for the joy set before him." Which means he ran out of desire. To use the familiar phrase, his heart was fully in it.[2]

Why was His heart fully in it? Because union means everything. It changes everything. It's two becoming one. We see it in marriage. We see it in sexual union. We see it in the Trinity. But so often we fail to remember it. This is perhaps the greatest travesty—we anchor ourselves to the idols that cannot and will not provide what is necessary because we forget union isn't something we feel; it is something we are meant to partake of.

Hannah Whitall Smith says it this way in *God Is Enough:*

> We all know that our emotions are untrustworthy
> and are largely the result of our physical condition
> or our natural temperaments. It is a fatal mistake,
> therefore, to make them the test of our oneness
> with Christ.[3]

Jesus said this in John 14:17: "But you know him [the Holy Spirit], for he lives with you and will be in you." And then in verse 20: "On that day you will realize that I am in my Father, and *you are in me, and I am in you*" (emphasis added).

Hannah Whitall Smith goes on to say:

> Do you understand the words "one with Christ"?
> Do you catch the slightest glimpse of their mar-
> velous meaning? Does not your whole soul begin
> to exalt over such a wondrous destiny? It seems
> too wonderful to be true that such poor, weak,
> foolish beings as we should be created for such an
> end as this; yet it is a blessed reality.[4]

Do you understand this glorious mystery, beloved? Do you ponder it in your heart? Has it made a differ- ence in your life, or do you simply observe it from a dis- tance, hesitant to enter in? The answer to these questions means everything, because the power of presence is only made possible through union, and how we respond to that union will determine everything else in our lives.

Passion and desire flow from such intimacy. Think

about your closest relationships. Are you passionate about them? Are they filled with the anticipation they once were? Are they filled with longing? Do you look forward to being in the presence of those you love? Are you known by those closest to you? If most of us are honest, we aren't too passionate about much by the time we wash up on the shores of midlife. We've settled into ruts and lived way too long in the dullness of routine.

"So what?" you may say. "I'm tired, and it takes too much energy and effort to generate that kind of desire." Well, consider this: When you allow your passion to die, so does your heart. You settle for giving yourself away to mediocrity. If you're tired of living on the sidelines, if you want to light a fire again in your soul, you have to tap into the flow of God's life within you. You have to find a way to access God and light the spark that will reignite that which has long lain dormant.

AN ENCROACHING WEARINESS

Elijah is another biblical character who knows exactly what we're facing in our struggle. Here is a man who was absolutely shot from so much action. To say he was tired of the fight would be the understatement of the century. God had called him to vigorously oppose Baal worship and idolatry in the land of Israel, and to do that, he had to go up against the wicked Queen Jezebel and King Ahab. Jezebel was notorious for killing prophets. There had been no rain in Israel for three years because the people had turned their backs on God, and in His judgment He brought a severe drought. All of Israel was suffering. Elijah summoned the king and 850 prophets of Baal and Asherah to Mount Carmel for a showdown between the false gods and the true God of Israel. God performed an amazing miracle through the prophet that day, but Elijah's victory made Jezebel more determined to kill him. He was forced to run for his life. Scripture says, "He came to a broom bush, sat down under it and prayed that he might die. 'I have had enough, LORD,' he said. 'Take my life; I am no better than my ancestors'" (1 Kings 19:4).

As we reflect on the story of Elijah, it's important to notice how the angel sent to minister to him addressed his physical needs first. The angel didn't start giving him a theological lecture. He didn't try to convince Elijah that his feelings of discouragement and despair were silly. He didn't tell Elijah that God had more work for him to do and that it wasn't time for him to die. He just met Elijah right where he was and provided what he needed most in that moment: nourishment and sleep for the journey that lay before him.

Elijah didn't ask for the silence and the solitude he needed. He didn't willingly move toward it. He entered into it out of complete exhaustion and deprivation. That's why he fell asleep under the tree.

We would be wise to reflect on this in our own lives, and be curious about why we are so unwilling to surrender to the rest that is most needed. What are we trying to do? Why are we afraid to be still? Why aren't we able to clear the time from our schedules to be with ourselves and with God? The answers to those questions will reveal a lot about our hearts.

Elijah experienced a profound sense of emptiness after his encounter on Mount Carmel. It caused him to despair of life. When we get to this point, it's no longer about being physically tired; it's about everything in our lives converging into a form of inner chaos that we can no longer ignore. We come face-to-face with the truth that all our attempts at performing and trying harder to prove our self-worth are so deeply rooted, we are terrified at how we will function without them. So like Elijah, we run to escape or avoid.

Others may notice our running and our frenetic motivation to always be in motion because that's what we have known as familiar. We believe if we do stop to consider why we're running, if we get alone with our emptiness, we'll be totally undone. This kind of emptiness is fueled not only by years of constant running but also by years of not paying attention to our hearts. What if we stopped? What if we slowed down? What if we paid attention to the dead tired we're feeling and were willing to explore it before God?

The pain buried deep within us is clamoring for attention, clamoring to be heard, clamoring to escape, but our fears keep pushing it down. It's time for us to be honest about our neediness with the only person who can actually do something about it: Jesus.

WHEN GOD SHOWS UP

Without connecting our hearts to the spiritual source of life, we leave ourselves open to spiritual dehydration because we can only be transformed through connection with God. Remember, as a result of Adam's sin we lost spirit life. We lost what we were made for, and what we were made for only happens as we encounter God. That's what Elijah was searching for, and he was willing to enter into the wilderness to find it because he believed only God could heal the disillusionment in his life.

But there were no quick fixes for Elijah any more than there is a quick fix for Jesse or for you or for me. Elijah had to wander in the desert for forty days and forty nights (1 Kings 19:8), and God was silent.

Life requires that we wait, sometimes solo. The very thought of it can undo us, especially if we're suffering. We wait for a diagnosis. We wait to heal from the loss of a betrayal. We wait to recover from the death of someone we love. We wait for a prodigal son to return home. We wait for a marriage to be restored. Those are the biggies. Then there's the more mundane waiting: We wait in lines, we wait at traffic lights, and we wait to catch a flight. We wait to be promoted, we wait until we have enough money to buy what we want, and sometimes we wait for a second chance.

Then when we least expect it, God shows up. He invites us into a deeper sense of self-awareness, the thing we have been running from all along. But there in that place we can take the time to invite Him in and answer the questions He places before us.

That's what He did with Elijah. He asked a simple question that got Elijah thinking: "What are you doing here, Elijah?" The question penetrates his soul. He shares his dilemma with God, and it's there that he recognizes he has lost heart. He was discouraged and disillusioned, and he had lost faith. He didn't know this truth about himself until he got away from the city and entered into stillness. Ruth Haley Barton echoes the importance of this step in her compelling book *Invitation to Solitude and Silence:*

> The willingness to see ourselves as we are and to name it in God's presence is at the very heart of the spiritual journey. But it takes time, time to feel safe enough with ourselves and with God to risk exposing the tender, unfinished places of the soul. We are so accustomed to being shamed or condemned in the unfinished parts of ourselves that is hard to believe there is a places where all of who we are—the good, the bad and the ugly—will be handled with love and gentleness. Solitude is just such a place, but it takes time to learn to trust it. This is part of what the waiting is about.[5]

CHOOSING STILLNESS

The journey of soul care requires a daily filling of the presence of God. It requires a deliberate "entering in" to what God has promised: "You will show me the path of life; in Your presence is fullness of joy; at Your right hand are pleasures forevermore" (Ps. 16:11, NKJV). This is the only way to keep the Impostor and his accompanying exhaustion at bay—by realizing that life, joy, peace, and pleasure are only to be found in one place: Christ Jesus.

However, just because we've learned that truth and removed the masks of the Impostor, that doesn't mean we won't be tempted to default to our old ways to manage life. Relapse is not only possible; it's highly probable due to the nature of our flesh.

Not only are we prone to wandering, but we are also prone to living busy, frenetic lives—and busyness distracts us from our one true love. It seems as though the only thing that moves us to stillness is sickness, suffering, or desperation.

To begin the journey of entering into the presence of God, we are required to notice the condition of our hearts. This can be terrifying because the more self-aware we become, the more shame and emptiness seem to settle into our souls. Like Jesse, we've made life work by wearing the masks we needed to keep the false self under wraps. Once we're exposed, we're scared that all our pretending hasn't left much of a self to identify with anymore. Like Jenni Schaefer, we've lived so long with our "Ed" that we don't know who we will be without him.

What we need to do at this impasse is surrender our rights to the idea of trying to figure things out in our minds. All those meddlesome "whys" and "if onlys" that plague us need to be relinquished for something deeper. Ruth Haley Barton agrees:

If we are able to notice the difference between what goes on in the mind and what goes on in the heart, we might eventually acknowledge that our mind is tired of trying to hold everything together, figure everything out, make something happen. We might notice the way our wordy prayers keep us working at things in our head rather than allowing our mind to rest in God's heart of love, where his good intentions toward us can make themselves known. If we are able to stay with our frustrations long enough and not give up, we may begin to suspect that the things that most need to be known and solved and figured out in our life are not going to be discovered, solved or figured out at the thinking level anyway. The things we most need to know, solve and figure out will be heard at the listening level, that place within us where God's Spirit witnesses with our spirit (Rom. 8:16).[6]

For Jesse and for you and me, that means giving up on finding answers, at least in part. It means being open to the possibility of receiving from God what truly needs to be discovered. Jesse knew the busyness in her life protected her from answering the deep questions of the heart. I asked her to consider that what she didn't know about herself could be a big part of what had been keeping her stuck, so she decided to unwind what was driving a life of constant running.

It wasn't some huge revelation. It actually showed up in every area of her life—she just never wanted to admit it. She had been so conditioned to live a life of "looking the part" that she didn't realize how insecure she really was. Even though she seemed to have it all, it was never enough. She always wanted more because she was using the wrong things to feel full. The "more" she really needed was Jesus.

I asked her if she had any resistance to practicing the spiritual disciplines of silence and solitude. She confessed she was afraid of them—afraid of facing herself because she wasn't sure what she would find if she actually looked beneath the externals. I assured her that listening to her fears was a good thing because it made space for her to hear what God was saying to her. That was the problem: she was terrified of what might be revealed.

Dallas Willard said:

> Silence is frightening because it strips us as nothing else does, throwing us upon the stark realities of our life. It reminds us of death, which will cut us off from this world and leave only God and us. And in the quiet, what if there turns out to be very little between God and us?[7]

Silence and solitude make us uncomfortable because we feel out of control—but that's just where God wants us. Maybe we're afraid He won't show up. Or that He won't give us answers. Or that we won't like the answers He gives to the questions we ask.

RECONDITIONED TO WAIT

The key is learning to wait. And waiting is maddening because we're impatient. We've been conditioned that way by the world. Instant messaging. Instant breakfast drinks.

Instant chat. High-speed Internet. Instant streaming of movies and music. We don't have to wait for anything anymore—and it's killing us.

We're so busy expecting results that we don't have a clue what waiting can produce in us. The truth is, we can learn from waiting if we begin to think differently about it and if we condition our hearts to that which is most necessary: listening and learning.

Even Jesus waited. He waited to be about His Father's business. He waited before He went to raise Lazarus from the dead. He waited to turn the water into wine. He waited for Judas to betray Him. He waited to hear the Father's voice, and He waited to die.

And in the waiting He modeled some things for us that can change our lives, if we're willing to embrace a different perspective. Jesus modeled dependence on His Father. He modeled the power of prayer. He modeled stillness. He modeled how to surrender rights. He modeled how to handle being misunderstood, rejected, and humiliated. He gave us a real-life example of how to live and wait.

Sure, waiting can be maddening, but it drives us to dependence as nothing else can. The question is: Whom shall we depend on in our waiting, God or ourselves?

Jesse confessed she did not wait wisely. She was more interested in knowing the outcome. She was impatient because she wanted to know the answers. She was uncomfortable not knowing the whys, and when she did all those things, she really wasn't trusting. I asked her what it would look like for her to stop doing and instead to trust God to work things out in His timing and in His way.

Any relationship that's worth something requires waiting. We wait for someone special to love us. We wait to see if we'll be forgiven. We wait for an apology from someone who has wronged us. We wait for a wayward child to come home. Waiting is risky because we're afraid we won't receive what we're waiting for. But in the midst of the waiting, Jesus promises to be there. He says, "I am with you always" (Matt. 28:20), "I am near" (Phil. 4:5), and "I will comfort you" (see 1 Peter 5:7) . The power of His presence in the waiting sees us through the fear.

THE WAITING PRIZE

But let's learn from the example of Jesus. He risked everything as He waited to go to the cross. He was undone in the flesh, so much so that He sweated great drops of blood from the anxiety He experienced. He asked the Father for another way. He waited for the answer. God said it had to happen this way for the Scriptures to be fulfilled.

But something amazing happened in the waiting that night in Gethsemane. Jesus went from sweating drops of blood on His knees before God to crushing the head of the serpent. How did this happen? In the stillness of the waiting He heard His Father's voice. It empowered Him. It strengthened Him. It would see Him through what lay ahead.

Now Jesus is doing the asking. He's doing the inviting.

He's saying to us, "Come to Me. Sit and wait with Me, and I'll show you what I can do with your heart." He's saying *enter in.*

In the Book of Hebrews the apostle talks about this idea of entering in as it relates to Sabbath rest. He reminds us we have a promise left to us by Christ of entering into His rest (Heb. 4:1–3). He is telling us that when we practice the presence of God, we enter into our covenant relationship with Christ, our blessed union with Him and our communion with God through Christ. In this state we can embrace the pardon of our sin, the peace of our conscience, the joy of the Holy Spirit, and the increase of God's grace, and we can immerse ourselves in God until we are prepared to rest with Him in heaven.

This is the heart of union. This is how the disciplines of the Spirit help us enter into God's presence as well as His peace and rest. This, beloved, is what our souls need—because if we're honest, all those years of running, pushing, and trying harder have worn us out. Just like Elijah, we're tired, and we need to press into that awareness and ask ourselves what the exhaustion is trying to communicate to us. Where is the weariness coming from? What is it saying about our core need? What hinders us from tending to ourselves? To our relationship with the Father?

We are so prone to beating ourselves up and reprimanding ourselves for not being able to shake off our exhaustion and get back in the game when the kind of weariness that we often feel, the kind that leaves us feeling sandblasted to the core, deserves some space and introspection.

Rest was a foreign concept for Jesse. To go there, she had to explore unchartered territory. She had to move from the comfortable to the unfamiliar. Rather than distracting herself, she needed to allow desire along with desperation, doubt, and longing to lead her to an inner experience with the Savior.

WALK INTO THE EMPTINESS

So far we've seen that the masks the Impostor gives us to wear temporarily keep us from experiencing the emptiness that threatens to drill down on our souls. The problem is the word *temporary*. To find ourselves, we have to find God, and sometimes the only way to do that is to walk into the emptiness that silence and solitude create.

Refusal to do so only prolongs the agony and shuts the door on God's work in our hearts. Elijah was willing to make the trek into the wilderness, but he didn't go alone. God was there all along, quietly guiding him and whispering his name. Elijah went into the wilderness empty, but he emerged full. He made space for God to pour out healing and restore his discouraged soul. There were no quick fixes, no get-out-of-jail-free cards, but a chance for Elijah to ponder the deep questions God was asking him.

Taking off our masks requires we confront some hard questions. It also requires we get honest with God. There's no sidestepping allowed here. If we want to find our authentic self, we have to dig deep and stop defending ourselves. We have to stand on the edge of the cliff and jump off, knowing the God we are anchored to will carefully set us in a safe place.

So, how do we begin the practice of silence and solitude? By understanding what we are actually doing along this spiritual path. We are asking for illumination from the Spirit. That means we wake up to what reality actually is. We are willing to see ourselves as we really are—without the masks. Next, we are willing to be stripped of all within us that is false—the false self.

Then we wait. But we wait with expectancy. We wait with longing, and we wait believing that God desires more than anything else to be found by us and to know us.

How to Step Into the Practice

I led Jesse in a few exercises to begin her practice of time alone with God, and you might want to try this too.

To begin, I asked her to settle herself in a comfortable chair and to take a few deep breaths to calm herself from the noise of the day. The place you choose for your time alone with God isn't important. Remember, Elijah was under a tree and inside a cave. The key is the attitude of your heart.

The next thing I asked Jesse to do was become aware of the condition of her physical body. What did she notice about her body? Was there any tension? Where was it located? Did she feel tired? Was there any heaviness within her? What did she need? Was she willing to ask God to tend to her physical needs? Could she sit with that and listen?

I led her in a prayer of gratitude for this time of rest before the Father. Each day as she began her practice, she was to first attend to her physical needs by doing her breathing exercises and the progressive muscle relaxation I taught her before she faced the deeper work of resting the mind.

After she had received what she needed physically, I instructed her to ask God how the noise in her life kept her from knowing what He wanted her to know about herself today. The key here is to just observe and not try and figure things out. This requires a nonjudgmental stance that allows thoughts to go by without demanding answers.

Jesse found this difficult, and I told her to bring that concern before God. What was difficult? What was scary? Was she willing to be patient and wait without any time constraints? Was she willing to surrender her right to know all the answers? Was she willing to wait on God as Elijah did?

"How do I recognize God's voice in the silence?" Jesse asked. "How do I know if I'm really hearing from Him and that it's not just me hearing what I want to hear?"

"You'll learn to discern His voice," I told her, "because it will give you that peace that passes all understanding. His presence will wash over you and fill you like you've never been filled before. He will guide you in all truth through the power of His Holy Spirit. You will experience a more authentic self—a freer self—because you won't need all the props to make your life work anymore. If your flesh creeps in and you miss Him, He'll be faithful to steer you back on course next time because His will must always be accomplished."

> "For my thoughts are not your thoughts, neither are your ways my ways," declares the LORD. "As the heavens are higher than the earth, so are my ways higher than your ways and my thoughts than your thoughts. As the rain and the snow come down from heaven, and do not return to it without watering the earth and making it bud and flourish, so that it yields seed for the sower and bread for the eater, so is my word that goes out from my mouth: It will not return to me empty, but will accomplish what I desire and achieve the purpose for which I sent it."
>
> —ISAIAH 55:8–11

LET'S BEGIN

The invitation to silence and solitude is a personal one. It will be different for each of us. It's birthed from desire—a desire to connect with what we were made for. When the heart yearns for something it cannot explain, only one thing is necessary: a filling of the spirit. Desire will lead you. All that is necessary is to quiet your mind and allow the Spirit to do the work only He can do in us.

"That's easier said than done," Jesse retorted.

I know. But I reminded her of all we had learned about training our brains and establishing new neuropathways. This is where the rubber meets the road for us. We have to *practice and embrace* being still. The question is: How strong is our desire to develop the inner life?

As much as we don't want to admit it, life doesn't offer us much that we can control. But we can control our thoughts, attitudes, actions, and beliefs. Jesse wanted to become a different person, and she demonstrated her ability to make significant changes in her life toward that end—changes that were empowering and life-giving. Incorporating the disciplines of the Spirit as a regular practice contributed enormously to her character growth and dependence on God.

I encouraged Jesse to practice, along with silence and solitude, some of the other disciplines of study, meditation, and contemplation. Cultivating these would take time. Because she was by nature rigid in her thinking and doing, I encouraged her to be flexible in her attitude with these practices. They were not meant to be a legalistic chore but a way of life to connect herself to the heart of God.

It's important for us to set aside regular time at the beginning of our day to invest in the process of whatever disciplines we chose. Like any other discipline we attempt to establish, once we are in a natural rhythm with it, we begin to look forward to it with anticipation.

I encouraged Jesse to begin by noticing the demands she allowed herself to be distracted with before her day began. She admitted that technology was her downfall. She had to consider how what she did at the beginning of the day set her mind. To make our time with God a priority, we need to make some adjustments to our schedules.

As you embark on your journey with the spiritual disciplines, you too must notice the distractions in your life that separate you from spending time with God and receiving the peace only He can provide for your weary soul. Remember, this is *your* journey with God. There isn't a formula for making this work. In the quiet God will lead you. Like Elijah and all the saints before him, you will find your way out of the wilderness because God is faithful to reward those who seek Him.

My time with Jesse had come to an end. She had a new life. A new hope. A new relationship with God she had never dreamed possible. The healing she so desperately needed had been so clouded by pain, she couldn't believe it was possible to find her way out of the black hole and have a different life—but God had other plans. He's in the business of redemption. That's His job.

Jesse was no different than you and I are. We will all come to a place where we face a dark night of the soul. None of us get out of here alive. But as we've looked at some of the great heroes of the faith, we get one message: God is bigger than any evil that can befall us. In Genesis 50:20 we hear Joseph say, "You meant evil against me; but God meant it for good" (NKJV). Can we believe that?

Our legacy will depend on how we answer that question.

CONSIDER THIS

- What have you looked to in order to find lasting contentment apart from the Father?

- Can you relate to the story of Elijah? If so, how?

- How free are you to ask God for what you need?

- Are you willing to follow Him even if the road to healing is painful?

- What distractions might you have to deal with to begin the practice of the spiritual disciplines?

- Do you sense any anger at God for your circumstances or for the story line He's written for your life? If so, can you pour out your complaint to Him? Why or why not?

NOTES

CHAPTER 1
THE SECRETS WE KEEP

1. Richard Harrity and Ralph G. Martin, *The Three Lives of Helen Keller* (Garden City, NY: Doubleday, 1962), 7.

2. National Eating Disorders Association, "Get the Facts on Eating Disorders," https://www.nationaleatingdisorders.org/get-facts-eating-disorders (accessed April 23, 2014).

3. National Association of Anorexia Nervosa and Associated Disorders, "Eating Disorders Statistics," http://www.anad.org/get-information/about-eating-disorders/eating-disorders-statistics/ (accessed April 23, 2014).

4. K. Hepworth, "Eating Disorders Today—Not Just a Girl Thing," *Journal of Christian Nursing* 27, no. 3 (July–September 2010): 236–241, referenced in Christine Roberts, "Most 10 Year-Olds Have Been on a Diet," *New York Daily News*, July 3, 2012, http://www.nydailynews.com/news/national/diets-obsess-tweens-study-article-1.1106653 (accessed June 23, 2014).

5. *Phantom of the Opera*, directed by Joel Schumacher, (Burbank: Warner Home Video, 2005), DVD.

6. Larry Crabb, *Fully Alive: A Biblical Version of Gender That Frees Men and Women to Live Beyond Stereotypes* (Grand Rapids, MI: Baker Books, 2013), 82.

CHAPTER 2
WHAT WE DON'T NOTICE CAN HURT US

1. Shakespeare, *Macbeth*, 4.3.209–210. References are to act, scene, and line.

2. Rita Schulte, *Shattered: Finding Hope and Healing Through the Losses of Life* (Abilene, TX: Leafwood, 2013), 39.

3. Trisha Gura, *Lying in Weight: The Hidden Epidemic of Eating Disorders in Adult Women* (New York: Harper Collins, 2007), 32.

4. Peggy Claude Pierre, *The Secret Language of Eating Disorders* (New York: Vintage Books, 1997), 76.

5. Gura, *Lying in Weight*, 29–30.

6.   John Trent and Gary Smalley, *The Blessing: Giving the Gift of Unconditional Love and Acceptance,* revised and updated (Nashville: Thomas Nelson, 2011), 1–2.

CHAPTER 3
THE SETUP

1.   Crabb, *Fully Alive*, 82.

2.   *Hope Floats*, directed by Forest Whitaker (Los Angeles: Twentieth Century Fox, 1998), DVD.

3.   Tim Clinton and Gary Sibcy, *Attachments: Why You Love, Feel and Act the Way You Do* (Brentwood, TN: Integrity Publishers, 2002), 24.

CHAPTER 4
THE SPINNING OF OUR SECRET SELF

1.   Jenni Schaefer, *Life Without Ed* (New York: McGraw Hill, 2014), 8.

2.   Erik H. Erikson, *Identity and the Life Cycle* (New York: W. W. Norton and Company, 1980), 49.

3.   Schaefer, *Life Without Ed*, 9, emphasis added.

4.   *Harper's Bazaar*, "Demi Moore and Amanda de Cadenet in Conversation," January 4, 2012, http://www.harpers bazaar.com/celebrity/news/demi-moore-talks-to-amanda-de-cadenet-0212#slide-1 (accessed April 24, 2014).

5.   James Masterson, *The Search for the Real Self* (New York: Free Press, 1990).

6.   M. E. Connors and W. Morse, "Sexual Abuse and the Eating Disorders: A Review," *International Journal of Eating Disorders* 13, no. 1 (January 1993): 1–11.

7.   Gura, *Lying in Weight*, xii.

CHAPTER 5
YOUR BRAIN ON GOD

1.   Andrew B. Newberg and Mark Robert Waldman, *How God Changes Your Brain: Breakthrough Findings from a Leading Neuroscientist* (New York: Ballantine, 2009), 3.

2.   Dan Harris and Enjoli Francis, "A Look at the 4 Ways Americans View God," ABCNews.com, October 7, 2010, http:// abcnews.go.com/WN/book-religion-examines-ways-americans -perceive-god/story?id=11825319 (accessed April 24, 2014).

3. Newberg and Waldman, *How God Changes Your Brain*, Kindle location 843.

4. Ibid., Kindle location 2271.

5. Ibid., Kindle location 1018.

6. Ibid., Kindle location 2049.

7. Barbara Bradley Hagerty, "Prayer May Reshape Your Brain…and Your Reality," NPR.org, May 20, 2009, http://www.npr.org/templates/story/story.php?storyId=104310443 (accessed April 24, 2014).

8. Daniel J. Siegel, *The Developing Mind* (New York: Guilford Press, 2012), 21.

9. Ibid.

10. Timothy R. Jennings, *The God-Shaped Brain: How Changing Your View of God Transforms Your Life* (Downers Grove, IL: InterVarsity Press, 2013), Kindle location 843.

11. Ibid., Kindle location 2271.

12. Newberg and Waldman, *How God Changes Your Brain*, Kindle location 2049.

13. D. O. Hebb, *The Organization of Behavior: A Neuropsychological Theory* (New York: John Wiley and Sons, 1949).

14. Siegel, *The Developing Mind*, 33.

15. *Bruce Almighty*, directed by Tom Shadyac (Hollywood: Universal Pictures, 2003), DVD.

Chapter 6
Our Unattended Sorrows

1. Stephen Levine, *Unattended Sorrow: Recovering From Loss and Reviving the Heart* (Emmaus, PA: Rodale, 2005), 2.

2. Peter A. Levine, *In an Unspoken Voice: How the Body Releases Trauma and Restores Goodness* (Berkeley, CA: North Atlantic Books, 2010), 45.

3. Ibid., 88–89.

4. Ibid., 86.

5. Geneen Roth, *Women, Food and God* (New York: Simon & Schuster, 2010), 92.

6. Ibid., 103.

7. John B. Watson and Rosalie Rayner, "Conditioned Emotional Reactions," *Journal of Experimental Psychology* 3, no. 1 (1920), 1–14, as quoted by Christopher D. Green, "Classics

in the History of Psychology," http://psychclassics.yorku.ca/
Watson/emotion.htm (accessed April 25, 2014).

CHAPTER 7
THE TRUTH ABOUT GOD

1. Bible Hub, "4561 *Sarx*," http://biblehub.com/greek/4561.
htm (accessed April 25, 2014).

2. Kay Arthur, *Lord, I Want to Know You* (Colorado
Springs: WaterBrook Press, 2000), 15.

3. MyRedeemerLives.com, "The Names and Attributes of
God: Adonai (Adonay) & Elohim/El/Eloah," http://www
.myredeemerlives.com/namesofgod/adonai-elohim.html
(accessed April 25, 2014).

4. BlueLetterBible.com, "The Names of God in the Old
Testament," http://www.blueletterbible.org/study/misc/name_
god.cfm (accessed April 25, 2014).

5. Cecil Murphey, *Making Sense When Life Doesn't: The
Secrets of Thriving in Tough Times* (Minneapolis: Summerside
Press, 2012), 61.

6. A. A. Milne, *Winnie the Pooh* (New York: The Penguin
Group, 1926), 60.

7. BlueLetterBible.com, "The Names of God in the Old
Testament."

8. Judson Cornwall and Stelman Smith, *The Exhaustive
Dictionary of Bible Names* (Gainesville, FL: Bridge-Logos Publishers, 1998), 126.

9. BlueLetterBible.com, "The Names of God in the Old
Testament."

CHAPTER 8
WHO'S YOUR DADDY?

1. Watchman Nee, *The Normal Christian Life* (Wheaton,
IL: Tyndale, 1977), 43.

2. Ibid., 43–44.

3. David Needham, *Birthright: Christian, Do You Know
Who You Are?* (Sisters, OR: Multnomah, 1979), 31–32.

CHAPTER 9
THE HEART OF THE PROBLEM

1.   Curt Thompson, *Anatomy of the Soul: Surprising Connections Between Neuroscience and Spiritual Practices That Can Transform Your Life and Relationships* (Carol Stream, IL: Tyndale, 2010), 215.

2.   Ibid.

3.   Dan B. Allender and Tremper Longman III, *The Cry of the Soul: How Our Emotions Reveal Our Deepest Questions About God* (Colorado Springs: NavPress, 1994), 200.

CHAPTER 10
REBUILDING THE WALLS

1.   John Eldredge, *The Journey of Desire: Searching for the Life We've Only Dreamed Of* (Nashville: Thomas Nelson, 2000), 35.

2.   Ibid., 37.

3.   Ibid., 48.

4.   Ray C. Stedman, "Nehemiah: Rebuilding the Walls," Ray Stedman Ministries, May 2, 1965, http://www.raystedman .org/bible-overview/adventuring/nehemiah-rebuilding-the-walls (accessed April 28, 2014).

5.   Ibid.

6.   Ray C. Stedman, "Don't Be Paralyzed—Get Organized!", Ray Stedman Ministries, January 15, 1989, http://www .raystedman.org/old-testament/nehemiah/dont-be-paralyzed --get-organized (accessed June 24, 2014).

CHAPTER 11
PRACTICING THE PRESENCE OF GOD

1.   Anne Morrow Lindbergh, *Gift From the Sea* (New York: Pantheon, 1955), 45.

2.   John Eldredge and Brent Curtis, *The Sacred Romance: Drawing Closer to the Heart of God* (Nashville: Thomas Nelson, 1997), 197.

3.   Hannah Whitall Smith, *God Is Enough* (New York: Ballantine, 1986), 116.

4.   Ibid., 117.

5.   Ruth Haley Barton, *Invitation to Solitude and Silence: Experiencing God's Transforming Presence* (Downers Grove, IL: InterVarsity Press, 2004), 96.

6.   Ibid., 72.

7.   Dallas Willard, *The Spirit of the Disciplines: Understanding How God Changes Lives* (New York: HarperCollins, 1988), 163.

A Healthy Life—
body, mind, and spirit—
IS PART OF GOD'S PURPOSE FOR YOU!

Siloam brings you books, e-books, and other media from trusted authors on today's most important health topics. Check out the following links for more books from specialists such as *New York Times* best-selling author Dr. Don Colbert and get on the road to great health.

FREE NEWSLETTERS
TO HELP EMPOWER YOUR LIFE

Why subscribe today?

- ❏ **DELIVERED DIRECTLY TO YOU.** All you have to do is open your inbox and read.

- ❏ **EXCLUSIVE CONTENT.** We cover the news overlooked by the mainstream press.

- ❏ **STAY CURRENT.** Find the latest court rulings, revivals, and cultural trends.

- ❏ **UPDATE OTHERS.** Easy to forward to friends and family with the click of your mouse.

CHOOSE THE E-NEWSLETTER THAT INTERESTS YOU MOST:

- Christian news
- Daily devotionals
- Spiritual empowerment
- And much, much more

SIGN UP AT: **http://freenewsletters.charismamag.com**

8178